THE SOLDIERS' STRIKES OF 1919

By the same author

THE SOVIET CONSTITUTION
MAN AND PLAN IN SOVIET ECONOMY
HISTORY OF THE USSR
PEACEFUL COEXISTENCE
THE SOVIET UNION AND SOCIALISM
THE MUNICH CONSPIRACY
A HOUSE ON CLERKENWELL GREEN
BRITISH FOREIGN POLICY AND ITS CRITICS
WHEN BRITAIN INVADED SOVIET RUSSIA

THE SOLDIERS' STRIKES OF 1919

Andrew Rothstein

To my father

© Andrew Rothstein 1980

All rights reserved. No part of this publication may be reproduced or transmitted, in any form or by any means, without permission

First published 1980 by
THE MACMILLAN PRESS LTD
London and Basingstoke
Companies and representatives
throughout the world

Printed in Hong Kong

British Library Cataloguing in Publication Data

Rothstein, Andrew
    The soldiers' strikes of 1919
    1. Mutiny – Great Britain – History – 20th century
    2. Great Britain. Army – History – 20th century
    I. Title
331.89'281'35500941   UB787

ISBN 0-333-27693-0

Contents

Preface		vii
1	**FROM WAR TO PEACE**	1
	War's End: The Soldiers' View	1
	Workers During the War	5
	Strikes and Strike Leaders	7
	Beginnings of a New War	11
2	**FROM PEACE TO WAR**	17
	Soviet Russia Under Attack	17
	The New Pretext	21
	. . . And the New Press Campaign	27
	'Demob Delays!'	30
3	**THE SOLDIERS INTERVENE**	37
	Folkestone and Dover	37
	More in Kent	40
	The London Region	43
	Sussex	47
	Hampshire	49
	The West Country and Wales	51
	Salisbury Plain	54
	Middle England	58
	The North	61
	Scotland	63
	Overseas	65
	France	69
	En Route for Russia	75
	Archangel	76
	India	81
4	**'THEY UNDERSTOOD NOTHING'**	86
	What the Newspapers Thought	86
	In the War Cabinet	91
	How Britain Demobilised	98
	What the Strikes Decided	99
Index		109

Preface

In January and February 1919 there took place in the British armed forces, principally at home, an extraordinary protest movement of strikes and demonstrations against their further retention in uniform, now that the war with Germany was ended. It had no parallel in history. There had been soldiers' mutinies as long ago as Cromwell's day: there was the sailors' mutiny in the days of William Pitt: each had ended in implacable repression and executions of the leaders. But the outbreaks at the end of the First World War, although on an immensely larger scale than those at Burford in 1649 and the Nore in 1797, were not treated as mutinies and were not suppressed in blood. They were resolute but peaceful strikes and threats of strikes, like those of the organised workers around them. They were the actions of men living in the age, not of militant Puritanism or of the excesses of the Industrial Revolution, but of modern large-scale industry and trade unionism. The soldiers who took part in them – nearly all coming from working-class families – had an even greater right than the yeomen farmers and well-to-do artisans of Cromwell's New Model to insist that 'on becoming soldiers we have not ceased to be citizens'.

For this very reason, the strikes were successful, and in their success they had a profound effect on British history. Almost at once the Government of the day – though it was one which had just played a leading part with its Allies in defeating the most powerful enemy Britain had ever faced – recognised that it could not resist the soldiers' demand for demobilisation. The memoirs of its political and military leaders, the records of its Cabinet and of its military organisations, leave no doubt about that. Moreover, they show that accepting the soldiers' demand meant at that moment accepting a decisive change in British foreign policy: namely, in the policy of intervention in Russia. And when the British Government ceased to lead in that enterprise, none of its Allies could do anything but follow, faced as they were with much more dangerous internal opposition.

These soldiers' strikes were briefly mentioned in the war memoirs of Lloyd George and Winston Churchill, Sir Henry Wilson and Sir Douglas Haig. They were reflected in the debates at the British War Cabinet and of the Allied Supreme War Council. Historians and biographers of the personalities involved have as a rule mentioned them. But no documented account of the strikes themselves, and of their political setting, has yet been given, apart from one article in an historical journal and a few pamphlets dealing with particular incidents. Such an account is attempted in the pages which follow.

To have taken part in the movement, even in a minor way like the present writer, and to have been conscious at the time of its wider importance, one must of necessity be something like eighty years old today. That at any rate enables one to check recollections against obtainable records pretty well objectively: and in doing so, to be candid if not impartial.

Grateful acknowledgements are hereby made to the staff of the British Library's Newspaper Division at Colindale, the Public Record Office and the Imperial War Museum: their prompt and earnest co-operation made the detail of research not only possible, but pleasant. The same thanks are due to Mr Peter H. Liddle, creator and developer of the remarkable *1914–1918 Archive*, at present housed at Sunderland Polytechnic, and to Her Majesty's Stationery Office, for permission to quote from the Crown Copyright papers in the Public Record Office.

September 1979   ANDREW ROTHSTEIN

1 From War to Peace

WAR'S END: THE SOLDIERS' VIEW

By the end of the first week in November 1918, the First World War was rapidly coming to an end. After a victorious attack by the Allied armies in Macedonia upon the Bulgarian front on 15 September, and a rising of the Bulgarian troops ten days later (occupying their army headquarters and proclaiming a republic), the Bulgarian Government sued for peace before the month was out. In the second half of September, too, the British army in Palestine launched a successful offensive against the Turks, capturing Damascus on 1 October, and during the next four weeks the whole of Syria: on 30 October Turkey capitulated. During the last week of October, in turn, the Austro-Hungarian armies were heavily defeated in northern Italy, and on 27 October their Government asked for an armistice. The following day an insurrection in Prague declared the independence of Czechoslovakia, on 29 October the south Slav political leaders (Slovenes and Croats) proclaimed their independence at Zagreb, and on 30 October armed workers and soldiers seized the main government buildings at Budapest, installing a left-wing Government which announced Hungary's withdrawal from the war. The Austro-Hungarian Empire thus ceased to exist – an event rounded off by a revolution in Vienna on 3 November which established a republican Government. In this way all Germany's allies had been overthrown, and the Kaiser's Government stood alone.

However, despite mounting Franco-British-American attacks on the Western Front from mid-July onwards, Germany continued a stubborn resistance. Its government had given up all hopes of victory and, alarmed by reports of insubordination and anti-war demonstrations among its troops, began seriously thinking of getting the best possible terms from the Allies. In the last week of September, however, a series of successful Allied offensives broke through the biggest German defences along the whole Western

Front, driving the German armies back half-way into Belgium in the north and close to their own frontier in the centre and the south. The battles in October were still bloody: the British forces alone suffered 120,000 casualties (as Lloyd George recorded in Chapter 82 of his *War Memoirs*), the French and the Americans comparable numbers, while the Germans lost probably as many as all three of their adversaries put together. As the British Prime Minister wrote (Chapter 85), 'All the world was panting for peace. Yet for weeks the fighting went on'. As late as 19 October Sir Douglas Haig, the British Commander-in-Chief, told the London War Cabinet that the Germans could still hold defensive lines 'for some time after the campaign of 1919 commences'. By that time a new German Government of moderate Conservatives, Liberals and Socialists had appealed for an armistice (5 October); but only after the German navy at Kiel had revolted (3 November) and in the next few days popular revolts in a number of provincial states had deposed kings, princes and grand-dukes, did the German General Staff send an armistice delegation across the lines at Compiègne (8 November). Next day, with a general strike in Berlin, the Kaiser fled to Holland, and on the morning of 11 November a general armistice was signed.

In their memoirs of the First World War, Lloyd George and Winston Churchill described with sufficient eloquence the anguish of expectation of the British people during those last months, and the immense explosion of relief – the wild exultation, the cheering crowds in the streets of every town – when the news came on 11 November that the last shots had been fired on those fronts where the two great war coalitions had fought each other. Even the immense outpouring of blood, in which upwards of 10 million young men had perished, was temporarily pushed back into second place. The British dead by the end of the war (not counting those of her overseas contingents) totalled some 800,000, out of a population of 45 million, about 1·8 per cent. This was not the heaviest toll in soldiers' lives among the combatants. The French dead numbered, for example, 1,400,000 out of a population of 40 million – 3·5 per cent. Nevertheless, there were few families which had not lost someone near and dear to them. And it is noticeable that quite a number of the regimental histories of British units which were at the various fronts – particularly in the west – speak of much greater restraint among the troops in celebrating the Armistice than was shown by the civil population in Britain. The dead all around them, or recently left behind as the armies advanced, were a present and painful reminder of what victory had cost. Here are some examples:

> Strange to relate, there was no tremendous excitement ... Perhaps we were too weary in mind and body to grasp the significance of the stupendous news. Or was it that our thoughts turned at this time to those grand men who had given their lives for this great end? Whatever the reason, the fact remains that there was no enthusiasm in keeping with the event.[1]

> 'The news of the cessation of the hostilities which arrived at about 1 p.m. evoked no great enthusiasm';[2] 'There was no dramatic moment, no splendid enthusiasm and rejoicing as with the crowds who had spent the war at home'.[3]

> At home, throughout the United Kingdom, the news was received with uproarious and mad manifestations of joy: but along the road to Escalette on the morning of 11 November [and indeed along the whole of the Western Front], when the Great Silence fell at 11 am, there were no shouts or exultations ... None forgot the gallant and noble souls who had given their lives.[4]

> The fact of the conclusion of an Armistice is recorded in the diary of each Battalion – concisely and without comment ... It is strange that nowhere is mentioned the reaction of officers and men to an occasion of such moment. Possibly minds were incapable of grasping immediately such a stupendous fact.[5]

There is a graphic footnote to these last remarks in the Manuscript Department of the Guildhall Library in London:

> Nov. 11 Armistice signed with Germany. Order for cessation of hostilities received 1100. Brass band played at guard mounting for first time. Battalion employed under 513 Field Coy. R.E. on roads.
> 12 Weather fine. Work on roads continued.
> 13 " " " " "
> Received orders that 56th Division will form part of Army of Occupation.
> ...
> 17 11 45. Voluntary Church parade.[6]

The latter entry is, by the way, the first sign that something had changed in the established routine of the battalion.

At the Imperial War Museum in London there are the diaries of Mr A. Allwood, then an officer in the 7th Battalion, Shropshire Light Infantry, serving in France. On 11 November he wrote that, having heard the news of the Armistice,

> I went back to A Company and simply said: 'It is all over, boys.' They looked at me as if stunned. I don't think they believed it. Then Brazier [another officer] came along to verify it – still they couldn't take it in. However, when they fell in and were given the about turn, a slight cheer was raised . . . Their first reaction was to ask how soon they could write to their people at home to let them know they had survived. That is the way I felt too.

So also Mr D. Calcutt, then a rifleman in 9 Platoon, C Company, 2/16th County of London Regiment (Queen's Westminster Rifles), also in France, who records in the same collection that they got the news as the general drove by: 'Nothing great happens, we have no facilities for rejoicing.' A church parade in the afternoon was the main break in the monotony.

Quite similar, at first, was the feeling in one signals unit of the Royal Engineers, as remembered by Sergeant Guy Buckeridge, also in France:

> We were all too tired to appreciate what it meant, and there was no sign of enthusiasm at all. However a meal, and later a double rum issue, revived our dormant faculties, and by evening we gave expression to our feelings more exuberantly, I am sure, than the people at home.

Mr Buckeridge died in 1956; his account is also in the Imperial War Museum.

So is that of Mr G. R. G. Mure (Royal Field Artillery), who recorded that 'my only memory of Armistice Day is trivial'. Colonel B. H. Puckle (57th Battalion, Machine-Gun Corps), whose unit was near Lille, wrote on 12 November 1918:

> Things have been very quiet here, and I've seen no signs of rejoicing or revelry by night . . . People took it so quietly. I think perhaps it is because we have not collected our ideas yet, and haven't quite realised what has happened to us.

Major Thomas Stamper (B/62nd Brigade, Royal Field Artillery), describing his unit's march on the morning of 11 November, recorded that 'during the march the Brigade-Major informed us that the Armistice had been signed, and all ranks were quietly jubilant'. One younger officer, Second Lieutenant S. Horscroft (RAF), remembered that the Armistice was celebrated by the burning of an old German wagon with thirty-two gallons of petrol, and by some of his fellow-pilots later frightening people on the roads and at a football match by flying low. Even these exploits, of course, bore no comparison with what went on at home in Britain.

The four papers quoted are all preserved in Mr Peter H. Liddle's *1914–1918 Archive*.

WORKERS DURING THE WAR

Nevertheless, it would be quite wrong to imagine that after the first moments of rejoicing the civilian population felt any marked relief from the special hardships which it had suffered during the years since 1914. In fact, by the time of the Armistice wartime economic conditions had made social tensions almost unbearable: and they were accelerating, with clearly political consequences.

Taking the level of retail prices in July 1914 as 100, they stood at 218 in the summer of 1918 and at 233 by 1 November. Real wages in mid-1918 were 75 per cent of their 1914 level – the maximum reached in certain war industries. In January 1918 the cost of living as a whole, taking into account food, rent, fuel, lighting and clothing (according to the official *Labour Gazette*), was 85 to 90 per cent above the level of July 1914. At the beginning of 1915 the rise had been only 10 to 15 per cent. But by November 1918 it was 120 to 125 per cent up. As a consequence, and taking the nation as a whole, meat consumption in 1918 was only 30 per cent of the 1917 level, milk 16 per cent, butter 15 per cent, sugar 7 per cent.

What did this mean in everyday, non-statistical terms? One answer must be sought in the pages of the Labour and Socialist weeklies, which stood closest to the life of the British working people – notably the *Herald* edited by George Lansbury, the British Socialist Party's *Call* and Sylvia Pankhurst's *Workers' Dreadnought*. From the spring of 1918 there were queues numbering thousands to buy the rationed goods – bread (and very poor bread it was), sugar, potatoes. Severe shortages occurred from time to time long before rationing began. Soldiers' wives were living on beggarly separation allowances, or getting low wages in munition factories, which undermined their health and that of their families. As a result a particularly virulent epidemic of 'Spanish 'flu' raged in the last months of the war – it was common to all countries where there had been an organised lowering of living standards to pay for the war – which carried off 7000 in Britain in the first week of November alone.

On the other hand, vast fortunes were made by many capitalists – those 'hard-faced men' who filled the benches on the Coalition (Lloyd George's) side of the House of Commons after the General Election in December 1918, and who 'looked as if they had done very well out of the war', as political satire put it. A Liberal peer, Lord Buckmaster, speaking in the House of Lords on 18 February 1919 pointed out that they had made 'the most amazing profits Britain ever witnessed – over £400 million made owing to the war . . . and in excess of profits made before the war'. A Liberal economist, L. G. Chiozza Money, who held an important post in the Ministry of Shipping during the war, wrote in 1919 in his *Fifty Points About Capitalism* that they made

> huge profits out of exporting commodities which we ourselves had good need to put into stock against the terrible submarine danger . . . The British people ran short of tea in the War because British profiteers sent it out of the country . . . Commercial men were sending out of the country for profit, in spite of the deadly peril of the times, food (fats) which we sorely needed ourselves . . . If the war had not occurred, the profits of shipowners in the first two years would probably have been less than £20 million. But as a consequence of the war, the actual profits realised by the shipowners amounted to about £300 million.[7]

Again, the average divided in the cotton-spinning industry was $6\frac{7}{8}$ per cent in 1914 and $16\frac{1}{4}$ per cent in 1918; in the engineering industry, 'practically every firm had amassed huge profits during the war years'; the coal industry's average profits rose from £15.5 million in 1914 to £23 million in nine months of 1918; net profits of the English banks went up from £9.1 million in 1914 to nearly £12.6 million in 1918[8] and British shipping companies' dividends on ordinary shares (taking the larger public companies only) increased from 7.9 per cent in 1914 to 13.1 per cent in 1918.[9]

What these figures stood for was reflected in the Socialist (but not only Socialist) press of the time – the shameless flaunting of luxurious living at expensive restaurants and country houses, the costliest fashions in clothing, furs and jewellery, no queues for food at the great stores for the rich, strawberries sold at 32*s*. a pound and plums at 1*s*. each: while coal had to be queued for in tiny quantities by the workers, unpunished cases of coal being delivered in taxicabs to the rich, 'rightly revelling in the West End of London', as the *Call* had written in April 1917.

Contrasts like these were a constant subject of protest at working-class meetings and – so far as fear of the censorship allowed – in the Socialist press. In other ways, too, as William Gallacher recalled in his reminiscences. Describing the songs at a meeting of 2500 shop stewards and factory representatives in the City Hall, Glasgow, on 28 January 1918 to hear Sir Auckland Geddes, the Minister in charge of manpower for the war, Gallacher quoted the chorus of a song then popular in the big industrial centres:

> Go to the war, workers, go to the war,
> Heed not the Socialists, but wallow in gore;
> Shoulder your rifle, worker, don't ask what
>   it's for,
> Let your wife and children starve, and go to
>   the war.[10]

These feelings were not unknown to the young men of the working class serving in the armed forces, even though they percolated very slowly through the filter of the censors and the general press.

STRIKES AND STRIKE LEADERS

What could not be concealed, however, was the strike movement which began soon after the war began, in spite of the pleadings, prohibition and threats of the Government and the press, the great majority of the trade union leaders and most Labour MPs. Except for certain miners' unions, the movement from the first was under 'unofficial' leadership, that of shop stewards. In 1915 a Munitions Act was adopted under which workers could be fined or jailed by special tribunals for (1) leaving their jobs without their employers' permission, (2) refusing to take a new job if they were dissatisfied with the pay, and (3) taking action at work which could result in 'restricting production'. Nevertheless, by July 1916 over 1000 workers had been convicted for participating in fifty-six strikes, and over 10,000 in all had been jailed or fined for breaches of the Act.[11] The works already cited – by William Gallacher and Wal Hannington – as well as other memoirs by rank-and-file workers' leaders of the time like Harry Pollitt, Tom Bell, Robert Stewart, provide the most convincing descriptions of how the movement developed.

After 1916, moreover, the strike movement grew in industry, as the figures in the official *Abstract of Labour Statistics* show (see Table 1.1).

TABLE 1.1   Growth of the strike movement in industry 1916–18

	1916	*1917*	*1918*
Disputes	532	730	1165
Strikes (000)	276	872	1116
Working days lost (000)	2446	5647	5875

SOURCE
18th Abstract of Labour Statistics, 1918

From the spring of 1918, too, just when battles on the Western Front were at their fiercest, the strikes grew bigger and bigger, as district and national leaderships began to be drawn into action, often unwillingly. In May, 50,000 miners and 17,000 engineers and shipbuilders struck; in June, 10,000 iron and steel workers; in July, nearly 100,000 workers in various war industries, notably engineers at Coventry, Birmingham and other industrial centres; in August the figure was 225,000, including 60,000 coal miners, nearly 20,000 London passenger transport workers and 14,000 London policemen and in September dockers, shipbuilders, aircraft workers, cotton spinners, railwaymen – 205,000 in all. The movement swelled in October and November.

These events did not mean, of course, that at any one time the vast majority of the British working class were engaged in industrial struggle, but the economic and social consequences of the war did successively bring more and more substantial sections into such struggle, however loyal their support for the war itself. Yet the memoirs of Lloyd George and Churchill echo the mounting condemnation of one union after another for its unpatriotic conduct in the last months of the war, by all the organs and supporters of authority.

Foremost among the organisers of these struggles, whether shop stewards or local trade union officials, were the more active members of the various small Socialist parties which then existed, who had been opposed to the war in principle from the very beginning. Yet even many of these were very far as yet from conceiving that the industrial struggles could become steps to revolution. 'We had a supreme contempt for the parliamentarians, having at that time no understanding of the importance of revolutionary parliamentarism as a means of combating reformism and stimulating the workers in the struggle for the overthrow of capitalism. We left the field clear for the reformists,' wrote William Gallacher of the great strike on the Clyde in 1918 in which he himself was an outstanding leader.[12] 'For a long time we were as men groping in a jungle on a moonless night,' wrote T. A. Jackson of a period when he was working as storekeeper in an engineering workshop:

> It was really surprising how thick the 'fog of war' became: how little we knew of what was happening in other parts of the country . . . The shop stewards and Workers' Committee movement began slowly to crystallise into the powerful instrument of militancy it became.[13]

A packed conference of delegates from workshop committees, trade unions and Socialist societies met in Leeds in June 1917, inspired by the Russian Revolution, and resolved to set up a 'Workers' and Soldiers' Council' for Britain. As T. A. Jackson wrote:

> Unfortunately we were not sufficiently on our guard to prevent Ramsay Macdonald, Philip Snowden and others from their stable – who all made bold 'Leftist' speeches – from getting elected to the controlling committee . . . The result was (as might have been foreseen) that the Workers' and Soldiers' Council for Britain . . . did nothing, with unshakable resolution, just when action was needed.

The workers who were not Socialists, yet fought like lions in their economic struggles, were naturally even less 'on guard'. Harry Pollitt wrote, of work during the war as a boilermaker:

> It was my experience time and time again that the workers you mixed with every day, who respected you, who listened to your arguments and suggestions, who you never thought could be swept off their feet by jingoism and flag-wagging, could by some incident or other be so transformed, though perhaps only temporarily, that they did not appear to be the same people.[14]

These considerable cross-currents in the rising mass of discontent were used by the Lloyd George Government and its supporters very much to their advantage. One method was to launch far-reaching promises of action after the war – 'homes fit for heroes to live in', 'hang the Kaiser!', 'make Germany pay', 'let the men who won the war win the peace' – and even the creation of a Ministry of Reconstruction, ostensibly in order to change Britain into a land of full employment, prosperity and social justice. Scarcely less effective was the propaganda of a demagogue adventurer, Horatio Bottomley, who in his weekly journal *John Bull* gave publicity to wartime scandals among the rich, seconded by some shopkeepers; to corruption among some officials and to ill-treatment of soldiers' relatives. All Britain was covered with his posters: 'Write to John Bull about it!', and tens of thousands did, while Bottomley combined his exposures with the most frenzied war propaganda and denunciation of strikes and Socialism. Anyone who served as a rank-and-file soldier at the time could testify to the almost drugging effect of Bottomley's campaigns.

At the same time, political repression was as severe at the end of 1918 as at any time since 1914. Hundreds of Socialists were in jail or internment camps for opposition to the war. Among them John Maclean, champion of the Glasgow workers and Marxist propagandist, who had been hunger-striking and forcibly fed since July. In mid-October 1918, the police raided the head office of the British Socialist Party to seize several thousand copies of *Lessons of the Revolution* by Lenin – a collection of articles written in 1917, actually long before the October Revolution. Some leading Jewish workers in the BSP, brought over in childhood by parents fleeing from persecution in Tsarist Russia and themselves educated as British subjects, were arrested and held for deportation, without any charges being laid against them. Sylvia Pankhurst, the suffragette leader, who after 1914 became a militant Socialist and editor of an anti-war Socialist weekly spreading the truth about Soviet Russia – the *Workers' Dreadnought* – was prosecuted for sedition at the end of October. Even on 5 November – the day after the Allied Powers had at last proclaimed their support of the principle of self-determination for subject nationalities in the coming peace – the House of Commons by a large majority rejected a resolution moved by the Irish Members which promised self-determination for their country. And the next day, although the collapse of the enemy armies showed the imminence of an end to the war, the Lloyd George Government refused to stop calling up for military service married men over forty-five years of age – an act whose significance will be seen later.

Therefore, when the cheering crowds poured out of the factories and offices and the largest and the smallest houses in the towns of Britain, on the stroke of the bells at 11 a.m. which announced the signing of the Armistice, it was to celebrate not only the end of the fighting, but also what most understood to mean the end of a régime of economic and social restriction, privation and discomfort (and what some believed must be an end to economic exploitation and political reaction).

But this turned out to be a delusion.

BEGINNINGS OF A NEW WAR

In the text of the armistice signed by the German and Allied representatives on 11 November 1918, there was a series of clauses not made much of even then, and now conveniently forgotten by most historians and journalists who write of 'Soviet plans for aggression against the West'.

Clauses XII and XIII laid down that all German troops were to begin to be withdrawn 'at once' within their own territories – with the exception that those in territories which before the war had formed part of Russia were to return 'as soon as the Allies shall think the moment suitable, having regard to the internal situation of those territories'. Clause XVI laid down that 'the Allies shall have free access to the territories evacuated by the Germans on their Eastern frontier, either through Danzig or by the Vistula, in order to convey supplies to the population of these territories or for the purpose of maintaining order'. Clause XXV stated: 'Freedom of access to and from the Baltic to be given to the Navies and Mercantile Marines of the Allied and Associated Powers'. Clause XXIX provided that 'all Black Sea ports are to be evacuated by Germany'.

These clauses represent the first open attempt to incorporate, in an international document, a kind of international sanction for the breach of international law effected by shelling, shooting, bombing and burning down of towns and villages of a country with which the Allies were not at war – the invasion of Soviet Russia, which had been planned within a few weeks of the revolution of November 1917, and was put into effect very soon after.

Apart from books dealing with particular aspects of this 'intervention', as it was officially called – to avoid using the ugly word 'invasion' – a few major works have sought to give an account of this undeclared war, all providing a mass of documentary material, most of it previously unpublished.[15] In 1918 the general public learned from its newspapers only the military facts (with, of course, a great many 'unfacts' customary at that time). The military facts may be summarised as follows. In February 1918, and again in April and May, British troops landed at *Murmansk*, the ice-free harbour in North Russia constructed in 1915–16. At the end of May and in the course of June, *Czechoslovak* troops recruited from among war prisoners captured by the Russian army in Austria–Hungary in 1914–16 mutinied and seized cities along the *Volga* and the *Trans-Siberian Railway*. In June British and other forces transferred by sea occupied *Vladivostok* in the Far East. In July, British troops coming up through Persia seized *Baku and the oilfields of the Caucasus*. In August, British, French and American forces occupied *Archangel*, the main port in north Russia, and more British forces arrived at Vladivostok. Immediately after the Armistice (November–December 1918) British warships entered the Black Sea and landed troops at *Novorossiisk* and *Batum*. In the *Baltic*, a British cruiser squadron began to co-operate with the German troops left in the territories along the coast, under the terms of the Armistice, to fight Soviet troops in Latvia.

Newspapers and official spokesmen did not trouble to conceal that everywhere the occupying forces acted in close co-operation with local anti-Soviet governments; indeed, at Archangel it was the invaders who set one up. Thus the clauses in the Armistice with Germany which are mentioned earlier were simply a means of ensuring easier and faster access to the places where the invading forces and their White allies were requiring reinforcements, munitions and other supplies for the war against Soviet Russia. What neither the newspapers nor the government told the British people was that these activities were the fulfilment of a deliberate plan for subsidising counter-revolution and ultimate intervention, adopted by the British War Cabinet as submitted by the Foreign Secretary, Mr A. J. Balfour, on 21 December 1917: that on 23 December the French Premier and Foreign Minister accepted it on behalf of France: and that on that very day the British, French and Italian military representatives in Paris (permanently there as part of the machinery of the Allied Supreme War Council) adopted a memorandum defining the different 'zones' of their respective countries' operations in Russia – an arrangement into which all the military activities described earlier (and others yet to come) fitted as into a jigsaw puzzle. The Balfour Memorandum[16] provided (1) that the British government should assure the Bolsheviks that it had no intention of interfering in Russian politics or supporting counter-revolution; (2) that it should at the same time help all the active anti-Soviet forces with money, officers and other agents; and (3) that 'this should be done as quietly as possible, so as to avoid the imputation – as far as we can – that we are preparing to make war on the Bolsheviks'. Even earlier than this (as a Foreign Office memorandum of 23 February 1918 recorded) the Cabinet at the end of November 1917 had already decided to provide money for anti-Bolshevik movements, and not to be 'deterred' if this produced 'a rupture with the Bolsheviks'.

For the majority of the British people, and even more of the British armed forces (except those sent to Russia), the 'imputation' referred to was indeed avoided during most of 1918, but for the Russians, both White and Red, and for the Soviet Government, it was a very different matter.

This is not to say that there were no voices of protest raised publicly in Britain. They were raised in the House of Commons by Mr Lees Smith, MP (14 March 1918); by Mr Joseph King, MP, and Mr Philip Snowden, MP (5 August 1918), and particularly in the Socialist press.[17] The British Socialist Party's weekly, the *Call*, in August carried several appeals to the labour and trade union movement to protest against the Allied landings in Russia, reporting a number of public meetings (at Glasgow, Wigan, Blackburn, Finsbury Park in London, Openshaw in Lancashire), at which such protests were adopted. After the landing at Murmansk a manifesto of the BSP Executive Committee was printed, in the *Call* of 29 August, setting out the text of a resolution protesting against intervention as war on the working class, and calling on the Government to abandon its policy which all workers' organisations were asked to adopt and make widely known. Within a week the resolution had been adopted unanimously at a meeting in the Sheffield Engineers' Institute and in the Rhondda Valley in South Wales, where on 9 September there had been a discussion on the resolution at the miners' District Committee representing thirty-two lodges, it was finally carried at the October meeting.[18] A similar ferment was going on in other main industries.

Those active in the campaign now opening required more information about Soviet Russia than could be gleaned from the almost unreservedly hostile daily press. To meet this need an attempt was made to provide a centre for such information. On 24 July 1918 a meeting of various Socialist and workers' organisations was held at Chandos Hall, Maiden Lane, London – the headquarters of the BSP – on the latter's initiative. It set up a 'People's Russian Information Bureau' (PRIB). The circular announcing this was signed by representatives of the BSP, the Workers' Socialist Federation, the Socialist Labour Party and the London Workers' Committee (shop stewards), as well as by S. Saklatvala, later the well-known MP. In September and October the PRIB circulated to the Socialist press some translations from *Izvestia*, the Soviet official newspaper. But in the main, during those summer months of 1918, when all attention was concentrated on the final battles of the world war, the PRIB, as it soon came to be known, made only a marginal impression on public opinion – and the same was true of the protests by MPs and trade union bodies.

It was only after the Armistice that a marked change in this respect began. In particular, workers at a mass meeting at the Holborn Empire, London, on 1 December, convened by a body of militant shop stewards – the London Workers' Committee – unanimously declared that they 'view with fierce indignation the appalling sacrifice of the members of our class involved in the continued campaign against the Russian Socialist Republic by the international capitalists, and demand the immediate withdrawal of the Allied forces from the country'. It called upon the National Council of Shop Stewards to campaign jointly with all Socialist and Labour organisations for a general strike, 'to compel the governing class to cease violating Russia'. The leaflet reporting this meeting announced the calling of a national conference of workers' organisations at the Memorial Hall in London on 18 January 1919, to promote industrial action if there was no withdrawal of British troops from Russia. It was this leaflet which first used the slogan 'Hands Off Russia!'

The conference was duly held, attended by 350 delegates, chiefly from trade union branches and trades councils. Wal Hannington and Harry Pollitt, who were among them, gave some account of the enthusiastic proceedings in their memoirs (*Never on Our Knees* and *Serving My Time*). Its consequences were far-reaching. But this was because great events had occurred, since the beginning of the year, which produced an extraordinary resonance for the decisions of the conference.

NOTES

1 *The Fifth Battalion, Highland Light Infantry in the War, 1914–1918* (Glasgow: 1921) p. 233.
2 H. S. W. Wenyon, *History of the 8th Battalion, Queen's Own Royal West Kent Regiment, 1914–1919* (London and Aylesbury: 1921) p. 256.
3 *The 10th Battalion, The Cameronians (Scottish Rifles)* (Edinburgh: 1921) pp. 153–4.
4 E. Wyrall, *The Somerset Light Infantry, 1914–1919* (London: 1927) p. 345.
5 W. W. Seymour, *History of the Rifle Brigade in the War of 1914–1918*, II (London: 1936) p. 355.
6 MS 9400, 'London Rifle Brigade 1st Battalion: War Diary on Army Form (2118).
7 Quoted by W. Hannington, *Industrial History in Wartime* (London: 1940) pp. 91–3.
8 Summarised in the Labour Research Department's *Workers' Register of Labour and Capital* (London: 1923) pp. 150, 166, 172, 180.
9 Labour Research Department, *Labour and Capital in Shipping* (London: 1923) p. 20.
10 William Gallacher, *Revolt on the Clyde* (London: 1936) p. 179.
11 R. Page Arnot, in his history of the Miners' Federation of Great Britain, *The Miners* (London: 1953), pp. 166–7, described the strike of 200,000 South Wales miners as early as July 1915. This work, and his later history of the Scottish miners, provide further material on the growth of the strike movement in this industry throughout the war. The 1 million miners had scores of thousands of their sons and other relatives in the armed forces.
12 Gallacher, op. cit., p. 205.
13 T. A. Jackson, *Solo Trumpet* (London: 1953) pp. 134, 136–7.
14 Harry Pollitt, *Serving My Time* (London: 1940) pp. 85–6.
15 Two of these works represent in effect a large-scale whitewashing of the invasion – the three-volume work by G. F. Kennan, *Soviet–American Relations*

1917–1920, and the two volumes by R. H. Ullman entitled *Anglo–Soviet Relations 1917–1921*. From the Labour and progressive camps which opposed the invasion from the outset, there are two substantial works in English: W. P. and Z. K. Coates, *Armed Intervention in Russia 1918–1922* (London: 1935) and Robert D. Warth, *The Allies and the Russian Revolution* (Durham, New Carolina: 1934).

16 Its full text may conveniently be found in Lloyd George's *War Memoirs*, II, chapter 71 (London: 1938). Other War Cabinet papers are quoted in R. Page Arnot, *The Impact of the Russian Revolution in Britain* (London: 1967) pp. 75–6, 113–14, 128–34.

17 The details may be found in *Hansard* for the dates mentioned, and more briefly in W. P. and Z. K. Coates, *History of Anglo–Soviet Relations*, I (London: 1943) pp. 138–40.

18 R. P. Arnot, *South Wales Miners, 1914–1926* (London: 1975) pp. 154–5.

2 From Peace to War

SOVIET RUSSIA UNDER ATTACK

Events in Russia had seemingly made it possible that Armistice in the west might coincide with restoration of peace in the east as well.

The Soviet Republic had come into existence a year before at a marked military disadvantage compared with its enemies. Wherever military units existed over the vast territory of the former Russian Empire – more than ninety times the size of the British Isles, but with only four times the population – nearly all the officers and a large proportion of senior non-commissioned officers were Tsarist in sympathy. The majority of the soldiers were anti-Tsarist, but had had nothing like the training which could at once produce efficient commanders. In remote areas like the Far East or the Cossack regions in southern Russia, the Whites controlled regular trained forces as yet scarcely touched by revolutionary ideas. Only at the Northern and Western Fronts and in the larger industrial centres like Petrograd, Moscow, Nizhni, Kharkov, Novorossiisk were there compact bodies of armed workers (Red Guards) and naval or military units which had gone over to the revolution. But Russia's enormous spaces and extremely thin network of railways, not to speak of her poor roads, made it extremely difficult to establish co-operation between these forces, and still less to make a unified army out of them. In the meantime, in these vast areas where industrial workers were a tiny minority, while the peasants had not yet had the experience of White rule, the anti-Bolshevik middle-class Socialist parties – Socialist-Revolutionaries and Mensheviks – retained considerable influence. They co-operated with the White officers in establishing local anti-Soviet governments (in the areas outside German occupation, twenty-two existed by August 1918), which suppressed 'Red' working class organisations and raised White armies.

In these conditions, the Soviet Government had to organise its

Red Army in the course of fierce armed struggle. It started with 200,000 volunteers in February 1918: by the beginning of May they had grown to 300,000. That month regular mobilisation of workers and the poorest peasants began in the main industrial areas, followed by the mobilisation of working peasants in other areas, so that by December the Red Army had grown to over 400,000. Its organisation, however, was of the most sketchy kind, and was having to be literally improvised as time went on.

A Supreme War Council was formed on 4 March; 'war commissariats' – local war departments – were set up everywhere, with power to recruit, train and equip, mostly out of local resources, on 8 April; general compulsory training for men between 18 and 40 was decreed on 22 April; a General Staff was formed on 8 May; all aspects of defence and strategy were concentrated in the hands of a Revolutionary Military Council (consisting of political as well as military leaders) only on 2 September and a General Staff Academy for training higher military commanders was established in October. Hasty training courses for lower commanders were created (thirteen in March had grown to sixty-three nine months later); and large numbers of Communists – almost exclusively factory workers – were drafted into the armed forces to act not only as fighters but also as 'commissars' (like the 'agitators' in Oliver Cromwell's army in seventeenth-century England). They numbered 100,000 in February and 400,000 in November, 1918. At the same time about 35,000 former officers and over 100,000 former senior NCOs were called up, and given responsible posts under the supervision of the commissars.

Thanks to these and similar emergency measures, scores of local voluntary detachments and military units which had gone over to the Revolution were gradually pulled together. At first they took the form of 'covering fronts', 'barriers' – more or less co-ordinated groupings of scattered units in the north (against the British, French and American invasion from the White Sea), in the south (against various White armies formed with British and French support by the Don and Kuban Cossack generals, and in the north Caucasus) and in the west (against White forces, backed by the Germans, set up in the Ukraine). Then, by the late summer, there were formed a series of organised fronts in the north, south, east and west, consisting of thirteen armies. In guns and munitions, in equipment and uniforms, even in food and medical supplies, these Red armies were markedly inferior to their opponents, who from the beginning of 1918 had been increasingly supplied, first, from German, and then from Allied sources.

Nevertheless, the Red Army had as the foundation of its morale the consciousness of its main backers – the workmen in the large centres and the poor peasants – that it was fighting to get rid of the exploiting classes, the factory-owners, landowners and bankers. By the late autumn, moreover, the main body of the peasants – those with no more than small family holdings – had discovered that wherever they came under the rule of either German occupying forces (in Belorussia, Ukraine and north Caucasus) or White generals co-operating with the Allied troops (the Czechoslovaks on the Volga, the British in the Caucasus, the Japanese in the Far East) the landowners were being restored to economic and political power. This, as Lenin pointed out at the time, meant that the sympathies of the 'middle' peasantry were turned decisively towards the Soviet Republic: and this, in its turn, made possible victories of the Red Army which had been inconceivable six months before.

By the end of October 1918 the White army formed in the southeast of European Russia by the Cossack General Krasnov had been twice utterly defeated in its attacks on the key industrial Volga city of Tsaritsyn (now Volgograd) and driven back over the Don. Attacks on Astrakhan, at the mouth of the Volga, by the forces of General Denikin coming from North Caucasus, were also beaten off. Further north, the Czechoslovak Legion had been driven right out of the cities it had captured up and down the Volga, and was retreating into the Urals on the borders of Asia. In the west, the troops of the counter-revolutionary Government set up by the Germans in the Ukraine were being heavily defeated by peasant partisans and workers' detachments (the pro-German Hetman Skoropadsky had to flee to Germany). In the north, the British, French and American forces coming from Archangel and Murmansk up the rivers which flow into the White Sea were being held in the dense forest, hundreds of miles from their objectives of Petrograd, Vologda and Kotlas (further east).

All this was accomplished in exceptionally difficult economic conditions. In the course of 1918 the main grain-producing territories – Ukraine, north Caucasus, the Crimea, the Urals and Siberia – were lost to central Russia. By the end of the year, out of 60 Russian provinces (i.e. excluding Central Asia, Transcaucasia, Poland and Finland), only 25 were left under Soviet government, and 15 of those were 'consuming' – i.e. they did not produce enough grain for their needs. As a consequence, food of every description was in short supply. The same applied to fuel and raw material for the main industries. Coal output in 1918 was barely 40 per cent of the prewar level; not surprisingly, since in the course of the year the great Donetz coalfield in the Ukraine, producing 10 million tons annually, was cut off, leaving only the small Moscow coalfield with less than 400,000 tons output. Only 1 million tons of oil could be brought up by rail from Baku, out of the 8 million tons available there. Reserves of iron and steel were down to a bare 600,000 tons by December 1918, and iron output was no more than one-eighth of the prewar figure. In October 1918 over 160 textile factories had to be closed down in order to provide minimum supplies for a few of the largest mills, and so on. A reflection of this situation was rapid inflation: in 1918 a semi-skilled worker's wages in Moscow were 2.5 times what they had been in 1917, while the price of flour on the free market had increased sevenfold.

Against these difficulties there could be an appeal only to the ordinary worker's consciousness of what was at stake in the civil war. It was exemplified by the vast and at that time unprecedented social reforms introduced by the Soviet Government – the eight-hour day, two weeks' annual holiday, free social insurance, equal pay for women doing the same work as men, maternity benefit at average wage level, prohibition of overtime and of the employment of young people under sixteen, the requisition of surplus housing for the workers, etc. It was these measures, however imperfectly applied, together with the organisation of the poor peasants (by a decree of 11 June 1918) to take over hidden grain stores and over 1000 million surplus acres of land from the richest (*kulak*) peasants, that ensured real mass support for the battles against the foreign invaders and their White allies. Arthur Ransome, in his *Six Weeks in Russia in 1919* (published in London that year) drew an arresting picture of these conditions.

This overall situation (as the debates show) was very much in the minds of delegates at the Sixth Congress of Soviets of Workers', Peasants', Cossack and Red Army Deputies which assembled in Moscow in November 1918, and which – three days before the Armistice in the west – adopted a resolution that it

> considers it its duty once more, before the whole world, to declare to the Governments of the United States of America, England,

France, Italy and Japan, waging war against Russia, that with a view to the cessation of bloodshed the Congress proposes the opening of negotiations for the conditions of peace.

The Congress's Central Executive Committee was instructed to take the necessary steps towards this end; and on 24 December Maxim Litvinov (then Deputy People's Commissar for Foreign Affairs), sent to Stockholm for this purpose, informed the Ministers of the Allied Powers there that he was 'authorised to enter into negotiations for a peaceful settlement of all questions making for hostilities against Russia'. This in fact was the fourth such offer since October 1918.

But it was not to be.

THE NEW PRETEXT

With the signature of the Armistice in the west, the bottom dropped out of the pretext most commonly used in 1918 for the invasion of Russia and interference in her internal political struggle. It could no longer be alleged that this was needed to bar the way to Germany's search for valuable Allied war material (stored in north Russia), or for foodstuffs (in the Ukraine), or to thwart her anti-Ally intrigues (in the Caucasus and Central Asia), or to keep her armed forces engaged in eastern Europe and thus weaken her war effort in the west. The British Government was now faced with the possibility of having to admit openly that its aim was to promote counter-revolution in Russia: that, as the War Cabinet had secretly decided on 3 December 1917: 'the policy of the British Government was to support any responsible body in Russia that would actively oppose the Maximalist [Bolshevik] movement'.[1]

Such a course, however, had the disadvantage of challenging working-class opinion in Great Britain, now freed from the influence of compulsory war propaganda (though not from the handicap of War Office censorship), discontented with the economic and social hardships inherited from the war years and already (as shown above) beginning to protest, here and there, against the use of British troops to overthrow the new authorities in Russia and reinstate capitalist and landlord rule. In the search for a new and plausible excuse, the Government therefore decided to rely on an appeal to sentiment – novel if not ingenuous. During 1918, thousands of Tsarist officers and senior NCOs had been enlisted in the anti-Bolshevik armies with the help of British or French money; British arms and equipment had been supplied for scores of thousands of peasants mobilised for the White armies; and thousands of Russian businessmen, large and small, and hundreds of Russian politicians and journalists, had thrown in their lot with the various White régimes. All these were now dubbed 'loyal Russians' (i.e. loyal to foreign governments and native counter-revolutionary generals) – and how could any British Government, supported by its very special kind of Parliamentary majority, described earlier, honourably desert them?

More and more, therefore, this line of argument began to come to the fore in public official propaganda as the new reason for continuing and extending military invasion and political interference in Russian affairs: while it was combined in private with undisguised determination to overthrow the Soviet republic.

Consideration of approaching problems in this respect began even before the Armistice was signed. On 18 October 1918, Sir Henry Wilson (Chief of the Imperial General Staff) brought in a report from Archangel that French infantry there were 'seriously affected by the possibility of an armistice on the western front', while the Americans also in that event 'would not fight offensively': and Foreign Secretary Balfour agreed that that would be a serious situation. The main justification of intervention had been 'to prevent German aggression'. But if British forces were now withdrawn from Russia 'we should suffer a serious loss of prestige, and should be letting down our friends'. General Smuts of South Africa was adamant that 'Bolshevism was a danger to the whole world': but Lord Robert Cecil (Under-Secretary for Foreign Affairs) feared that 'it might end badly if we tried to destroy Bolshevism by military interference'. However, he, too, didn't like the idea of abandoning the Whites 'to Bolshevik fury'. Finally it was decided that the Foreign Office, the Imperial General Staff and the Admiralty should prepare a paper on present and future policy in Russia. Meanwhile, the opinion of the French Government should be sought. These conflicting ideas, and the possible way out, recurred again and again in the immediately following weeks.[2]

During the discussions on policy, the invasion went on. A detachment of marines from HMS *Suffolk* joined the Czechoslovaks at Ufa in the northern Urals, a battalion of the Middlesex Regiment reached Omsk in Siberia, and British warships arrived at

Petrovsk on the Caspian. Arrangements were soon being made for a division to be sent to Batum on the Black Sea. And a proposal of a novel character was made by Foreign Secretary Balfour at the Allied Supreme War Council in Paris: that the German troops should hand over their arms to the anti-Bolshevik forces in the Ukraine and elsewhere.[3] This was too much for the French and others who had had the Germans on their soil, and it was rejected.[4] But this traditional hankering of some British rulers for friendly satellites to help in fighting their battles, practised since the days of the Duke of Marlborough, was not abandoned, as Marlborough's famous descendant was yet to show. 'Our real danger now is not the Boche, but Bolshevism,' wrote Sir Henry Wilson, Winston Churchill's close friend, on 8 November 1918.[5] 'We might have to build up the German Army, as it was important to get Germany on her legs again for fear of the spread of Bolshevism,' said Churchill himself on 10 November 1918.[6]

On 14 November 1918 Balfour reported on a conference about Russia which had been held at the Foreign Office the previous day. All British representatives 'on the spot' i.e. directly co-operating with the Whites, were in favour of an 'anti-Bolshevik crusade'. But such a crusade was impossible, because it would involve military operations 'of unknown magnitude'. To try anything in Russia proper was useless – but Britain ought to give every possible assistance 'to those elements in Siberia and south-east Russia who had stood by us during the war', and the western border states should also be included. On no account should troops be sent, said Lord Milner (Secretary for War). Lord Robert Cecil pressed for observing appearances: 'It would be fatal to let it be thought that we were committed to an anti-Bolshevik crusade . . . We should assist these people not because they were anti-Bolshevik but because during the war they had been pro-Ally'. But, with this explanation, south and south-east Russia should be rescued from the danger of 'anarchy', General Denikin should be helped, and an anti-Bolshevik government should be supported in Turkmenia. Lord Milner found another good reason: east of the Don and the Volga the governments opposed to the Bolsheviks 'were those which most closely affected the interests of the British Empire': they should be helped to resist 'a Bolshevik invasion from the West'. All came together once more on these principles, which as before involved helping everyone in Russia who was organising for counter-revolution: and they adopted a resolution, submitted by the Foreign

Office, providing in detail, region by region, (from Siberia to the Baltic), for such help.

Lloyd George, however, saw one danger. 'Here we had a great inflammable industrial population', and it was very desirable it should know that workers had suffered at the hands of the Bolsheviks just like the rest of the people. One and all, the other Ministers agreed with this proposition, and promised to collect information on 'Bolshevik excesses'.[7] Churchill's contribution, at Dundee during the immediately following election campaign (26 November), may be usefully quoted here as typical of the information with which the British people were accordingly supplied: 'The Bolsheviks hop and caper like troops of ferocious baboons, amid the ruins of cities and the corpses of their victims'.[8]

However, this sagacious propaganda was not as successful as had been hoped: during the election searching questions had been put to MPs by their constituents. Moreover, the Socialist weeklies, particularly the *Herald*, the *Call*, the *Labour Leader*, and the *Workers' Dreadnought*, were now making the campaign against the invasion of Russia a central issue. On 14 December the first-named had published a sensational and courageous attack on the government's policy in Russia by the British Consul at Archangel, Mr Douglas Young, who was on leave in Britain, and was incensed by the falsehoods with which invasion was being defended. At the War Cabinet meeting on 10 December, there were still Ministers who warned that to withdraw British troops 'would mean misery to thousands of people' (Lord Curzon), 'massacre would ensue' (Lord Milner), it 'would betray our friends in North Russia' (Mr Balfour).

But the very same people also betrayed a growing worry: 'A great many people in England objected to any British soldier remaining in Russia, as they could not get out of their heads that they were there solely for the purpose of fighting Bolshevism' (Curzon); 'the difficulty was really that our own people at home thought that the British troops were being used for the suppression of Bolshevism' (Milner). Lloyd George read out a letter from Bernard Shaw asking what British boys were doing in Russia. Later he added that if it was a point of honour now not to withdraw British troops from north Russia, the same argument might be used in twelve months' time – and even in four years' time. Finally, he warned that if British troops continued to be kept in so many places 'there would be discontent in the Army'. The origin of this new note of caution was blurted out by Chamberlain: 'The War Cabinet ought not to come to a decision simply because certain people asked questions during an election'! And so the decision was . . . to postpone a decision until the following week.⁹

Sir Henry Wilson in his military way put it bluntly in his diary: 'L G wanted to come away from Murmansk because he thought our occupation there was unpopular. *Again, all votes.*'¹⁰

But even when the General Election results, a few days before, had provided him with a thumping majority, Lloyd George continued to voice his doubts. 'No British troops could be found for the purpose [large-scale intervention] without conscription,' he said at the Imperial War Cabinet on 31 December 1918 –

> and if Parliament endorsed conscription for that purpose, he doubted whether the troops would go. Our citizen army were prepared to go anywhere for liberty, but they could not be convinced that the suppression of Bolshevism was a war for liberty.¹¹

In practice, Wilson continued, as Chief of the Imperial General Staff, to apply the provisions of a General Staff plan for 'Military Commitments after Peace Signed' (6 December 1918) – one division already under orders for Batum, a second probably required, neither to be withdrawn 'for a considerable time'; volunteers from the Regular Army to go to Transcaspia (Central Asia); no reduction in Russia (i.e. Murmansk and Archangel), and maybe 'some increase', up to one division.¹²

Thus, while Ministers had begun to argue among themselves as to whether the invasion of Russia was to continue, and maybe lead to further commitments – even on the new grounds of protecting the 'loyal Russians' – the military were proceeding as though there was no question about it. Indeed, Wilson recorded on 12 December that he had got the War Cabinet to maintain fourteen to twenty divisions for some time to come, in addition to the Regular Army, thus keeping up approximately a war footing.¹³

An indirect indication of their aims is the communication by Lord Milner to Sir Eric Geddes on 1 January 1919 that by 31 December only 108,000 men had been demobilised.¹⁴ Again, the War Office Directorate of Organisation recorded that the War Cabinet on 31 December had decided not to extend demobilisation to the British forces in Russia, although 'for the moment' more drafts were not to go there.¹⁵

A shrewd observer in London, the Tsarist diplomat K. D. Nabokov (formerly Kerensky's representative), summed up the situation – naturally from his own point of view as a spokesman for the Whites – in a message to his counterpart in Paris, V. A. Maklakov (Kerensky's Ambassador there), on 28 December 1918:

> The political obstacles to sending large Allied forces to Russia are tremendous, especially in England. All Radical circles and the Labour Party are carrying on a stubborn struggle for non-intervention, and the Government has to reckon with this very seriously. Moreover the troops themselves are thirsting for demobilisation.
>
> I know that during the election campaign just concluded the vast majority of candidates to Parliament encountered at the election meetings a sharply expressed opposition to sending troops to Russia, and this in turn is known to the head of the Government. It is undoubtedly true that Bolshevism was born of military defeat, and therefore is less of a menace to the victorious nations. But the four years of war, all the same, brought a certain uneasiness to the British masses, and a disorder which may arouse serious complications if the Government goes against the predominating currents of public opinion. Therefore the task of British statesmen is a dual one – to persuade President Wilson to make available American troops, who are less tired, and then to work out measures which can be taken by England without risk of protest from wide circles of the population. This help must take two forms – moral, expressed in recognition of, and close cooperation by the Allies with, the Omsk Government and the local organisations which are rebuilding Russian statehood: and material, by supplying armaments, equipment, food. In brief, it is necessary that by the efforts of the Allies the population of Russia should be convinced that, where there is law and order, there peace and prosperity reign.
>
> I am exerting every effort to have all this help afforded to us, and I can testify that on the part of the British Government there is a complete desire to meet our wishes.
>
> The big difficulty is the struggle with Bolshevik propaganda, generously financed from outside: for the propaganda in the so-called capitalist press does not convince those elements of the population who require to be convinced.[16]

... AND THE NEW PRESS CAMPAIGN

The government did its utmost to mobilise the press on its side through the 'usual channels', of which the war memoirs of Lloyd George and Winston Churchill (to take no other example) provide ample evidence. The press supporting the government responded loyally, not only by continuing to print a mass of horror stories about the Soviet régime, but also by taking up in its leading articles the new theme on which Ministers had decided – particularly while the General Election results were still to come.

Thus *The Times* at first prepared to switch its war propaganda from the theme of Germany to that of the Soviet Russia. With the British Navy commanding the Black Sea and Baltic ports, it wrote on 14 November, this 'should help to lift the clouds which still lie heavy over Petrograd'. And when the Labour Party in its election manifesto (polling was fixed for 14 December) condemned intervention, *The Times* thundered that 'it should be the business of every democracy to redeem [Russia] from the present tyranny' (29 November). Moreover, this in the eyes of *The Times* had become the supreme immediate task of the Allies. On 18 December the leading article declared that 'the great problem of all, for Germany and for the whole world, is: what is to be the future of Russia? Upon that the stability of the whole structure which the Allies are to build up will depend'. But the very next day the paper took up the new argument which War Minister Lord Milner had set forth in a statement issued on 18 December: 'We cannot betray our friends in Russia . . . We are in Russia in discharge of our moral obligations.' On 28 December, commenting on an entirely false rumour that a huge Soviet army was about to invade Poland, *The Times* opposed the suggestion that the attitude to Russia should be 'live and let live', asserting that 'there is a loyal minority in Russia whom we are bound to protect by every means in our power'.

On 19 December the *Daily Telegraph* had turned to the same theme as *The Times*. It wrote:

> The Allied Forces cannot in decency now retire and leave to the mercy of the Bolsheviks those Russians who have taken up arms and fought side by side with them . . . We have at present a war on our hands in Russia such as would have filled the newspapers at any normal time.

Most outspoken of all in its demand for full-scale war was the *Morning Post*. In a leading article on 21 December, 'The Rescue of Russia', the spokesman of the ultra-Tories wrote: 'We must face the fact fairly and frankly that we are at war with the Bolshevik Government of Russia. That Government has murdered British officers and cruelly ill-treated and imprisoned British subjects.' (In fact, not a hair on the head of either British officers or British civilians had been touched before the landing at Archangel in August: whereas General Maynard's forces at Murmansk and British forces in the Far East had been killing, or helping White Russians to kill, Soviet citizens months before.) 'It is the purpose of the Allies not to fight a Russian Government but to save Russia from the tyranny of an alien and traitorous camarilla,' continued the *Morning Post* (in fact, all the White generals with whom the Allies were by now co-operating stood for the restoration of the Romanov Tsarist régime, showing it by their wholesale massacres of workmen in particular wherever they held power). 'There is another reason which keeps us in Russia. If we evacuate that country, all the friends of the Allies now under our protection will be massacred' (omitting, of course, that it was by engineering the Czechoslovak mutiny in May-June and a series of risings in Central Russia in July that the Allied Governments had involved their 'friends' in action which put them in peril, and which they would never have dared to undertake without Allied money and promises of support). The *Morning Post*, however, did not wish to mince matters. It concluded:

> We ought especially to support our friends in Russia with all those modern weapons of war in which the Bolsheviks are deficient. The forces we send ought to be of the best quality, and of such strength as to ensure success.

And it repeated this stirring call on 31 December: 'It is time that the Allies should definitely declare war upon them, and despatch an expedition of sufficient power to destroy the whole criminal conspiracy.'

By this time the Government felt itself in a stronger position. By grace of the peculiar electoral machinery then existing, the votes in the General Election cast on 14 December were not counted until 28 December, and the results not published until the next day. Then it turned out to have been a real 'khaki election', assuring Lloyd George's Coalition of a huge majority, 472 to 130. Now it was possible to unmask the batteries. One by one the pro-Lloyd George press proceeded to the task of preparing the decisive operations against Soviet Russia: and in doing so it was even less restrained than before by respect for the facts.

On 1 January 1919 the *Daily Telegraph* fired the first shot: 'The Bolshevik Government is openly aiming at the expansion of that sphere [of its power] westward by force of arms . . . It makes no secret of its desire to infect as much of civilisation as it can reach with its own venom.' (What the paper did make a secret of was the explicit proposal of the Congress of Soviets on 8 November for peace negotiations, addressed to the five principal Allied Powers.) The Allied plan 'contemplates no action beyond what is required as a measure of international sanitation: it does not propose to move against the centres of Bolshevik power with force of arms'. (This was after the War Cabinet had for months been urging a junction at Kotlas or Vologda between the British forces in northern Russia, Kolchak's forces coming from the east, and the Czechoslovaks from the south, with a view to attacking Moscow!) Nevertheless, with a fine disregard for its own logic, the *Daily Telegraph* concluded by quoting as 'unanswerable' a speech just made by the French Foreign Minister Pichon: 'Any peace which allowed Russia to exist in a state of civil war with her present abominable government would not be a peace of justice.'

On 2 January Lloyd George's own paper, the *Daily Chronicle* – very reticent in the previous weeks – took up the tale. The 'Bolshevik menace' to the Baltic peoples should 'quicken the efforts by the Allies', wrote its editorial: citing as evidence that Bolshevism 'aims at overrunning and disintegrating the liberated peoples [Estonia, Latvia, Lithuania] before they have got on their feet'. Here, too, the paper ignored the simple facts: that in all three countries the native Soviet authorities set up after the defeat of Germany by their own workers and peasants were being attacked by a combination of foreign invaders – in Estonia, a Finnish expeditionary force supported by a British cruiser squadron; in Latvia, the same squadron co-operating with (and giving orders to) a volunteer corps of the lately enemy German army and in Lithuania, by a Polish army (claiming the whole territory as part of 'historic Poland') and units of the German corps.

On 4 January *The Times* in its turn denounced 'Bolshevist imperialism'. Ignoring like the rest of the press the repeated Soviet offers to open peace negotiations, it simply proclaimed that 'subversion' was the object of the Soviet Government, and 'all the protests against interfering in the internal affairs of Russia are beside the point'. Britain should be actuated 'by precisely the same motives as made us go to war with *Germany*,' wrote *The Times* in perhaps the most sinister terms yet used. True, it tried to hedge: 'There is no question *now* of landing the army of a million men which some are talking about,' it added. With the most confident contempt for the intelligence of its readers, *The Times* asserted that 'the question of intervention in Russia proper may stand over for the present' – when it was just that kind of intervention which British and Allied forces were practising in northern Russia, British warships at Sevastopol and Odessa on the Black Sea, British warships at Vladivostok and a British regiment deep in Siberia!

In short, war propaganda was being launched on a grand scale – when by uneasy admissions that 'for many months as yet, at the best, the bulk of our Armies abroad will have to remain on active service' (*Morning Post*, 9 December 1918); general demobilisation 'must wait until the political and military situation is sufficiently cleared up' (*The Times*, 12 December 1918); slowness of the aggregate rate of military demobilisation up to the present 'was inevitable', until the Government had 'formulated a clear plan for the future of British military policy' (*Daily Chronicle*, 1 January 1919). Plainly, the propaganda was aimed at justifying that same retention of the British army, on approximately a war footing, which Sir Henry Wilson had noted in his diary as his purpose – and his achievement in discussions at the War Cabinet – on 12 December. But now the aim was clearer: not only to provide for the armies of occupation in Germany, Austria, Turkey and Bulgaria, but also 'to destroy the whole criminal conspiracy' in the Soviet Republic.

'DEMOB DELAYS!'

Of course, the theme of the 'Menace of Bolshevism' inspired more than a few of the politicians' speeches during the election campaign in December: all the more because of the industrial unrest which hundreds of candidates were ready enough to see as the result of Bolshevik propaganda, proceeding somewhere, somehow – although in fact the still small campaign against intervention conducted by the Socialists and a section of the Liberal press had no links with the struggle for wages and against wartime restrictions on freedom of labour, while the trade union struggle described earlier very rarely took up, as yet, the question of the war on Russia.

But the pro-Government press itself was divided on that question. There were only two newspapers which, as a rule, a serving soldier could buy in the army barracks and camps at the end of the war, or which were sent out to soldiers on active service by their friends (apart from the local weeklies). They were the mass-circulation *Daily Mail* and the *Daily Express*, each owned by wealthy men with journalistic ambitions, if not wide journalistic experience, and Tory in outlook but not in party allegiance – Lord Northcliffe (Alfred Harmsworth) and Lord Beaverbrook (Max Aitken). In their search for a wide readership, they used the simplest words, the simplest style of presentation, in short sentences and brief paragraphs, most frequently used pictures – and invariably the last word in demagogic language, of which the most typical was to write 'Hun' when they meant 'German'! The *Daily Mail* on its front page daily called itself 'The Soldiers' Paper'. The *Daily Express*, unable to use the same title, specialised on collecting and voicing soldiers' grievances.

Very soon after the Armistice, these two newspapers began to complain of delays in demobilisation. They contrasted the speed with which whole categories of older soldiers were being sent home by the French military authorities, and entire transports full of American soldiers were leaving European ports for the United States, with the extreme slowness of British demobilisation. The principle on which this was supposed to proceed was known. 'Pivotal men' – i.e. those on whom entire industries, or sections of industries, or even important factories, depended in turning over from war work to civilian work – were to go first. With them could go 'slip men': those for whom there was a productive job waiting, and for whom their employer could send a 'slip' or certificate. But in each case it was the commanding officer of their own unit who had to give the order, and he was himself under the orders of a vast hierarchy of superior officers. Some categories of workers, like miners or railwaymen, were supposed to be released at once: others fell into later categories. This procedure of course provided vast opportunities for more bureaucratic delays: but the accumulation of delays, in the particular circumstances following the Armistice which have been described, quite easily led to the suspicion that the procedure and the delays were purposeful, aiming to keep back the soldiers for another war.

The editorials in the *Daily Mail* concentrated on the bureaucratic aspect of the delays. Answering a frequent theme of the propaganda in the 'big' newspapers about the need to keep up large armies because Germany was in danger of being 'Bolshevised' (the German sailors, workers and soldiers had, in overthrowing the Kaiser, formed revolutionary councils, in which there was a struggle going on between the majority Social-Democrats and the left-wing 'Independents'), the *Daily Mail* wrote on 22 November: 'We are convinced that nobody in this country, except a few financiers with extensive international connections, cares one continental fig how much Germany Bolshevises.' Soon it was conducting a steady harassment of the military authorities on the matter of demobilisation. 'Demobilisation is proceeding with a leisured step. It ought to go into a quick march . . . not in driblets but in a growing volume that will be evident to the man most concerned, the working man in the Army' (29 November); demobilisation procedure was 'a maze of red tape and official forms' (5 December); 'There is a stoppage in the pipes somewhere . . . The machine must be speeded up' (11 December): in order to make possible the speedier release of British soldiers, Germany's 2 million men still under arms should be demobilised (13 December) – these were a few characteristic comments, with scores of letters to the same point in the correspondence columns.

Only once during the eight weeks following the Armstice did a *Daily Mail* leading article attack Soviet Russia. This was on 19 December – the day after Lord Milner's statement, which the paper briefly summarised, under the heading 'Why Russia Stops Peace'.

But the *Daily Express* did not make even this concession to the official campaign for war with Soviet Russia, camouflaged as 'protection for loyal Russians'. On the contrary, while conducting an even more bitter attack on demobilisation delays than that of the *Daily Mail*, its attitude was set out in an editorial headed 'Russia Must Wait', on 22 November:

> It seems to be about time that we made up our minds about Russia. Shall we withdraw our garrison in Murmansk and Siberia, or shall we make them jumping-off places for restoring order throughout the whole of the old Russian Empire? . . . The *Daily Express* says quite frankly that the British Empire has for the moment done enough . . . We are not the schoolmasters of Russia or of other nations.

When the General Election campaign was launched, the paper made demobilisation the main theme of its editorials'. 'Here sits this great army, anxious to come back to work, waiting for some official to put his name to paper' (3 December); 'Men are urgently required out of the Army, just as urgently as they were required in it four years ago' (4 December); 'The whole of the demobilisation machinery is sticking, not from lack of goodwill but from lack of organisation' (6 December); Lord Milner (War Secretary) was responsible for 'the endless red tape formalities of the military authorities' (12 December); 'The military authorities, whether by design or by sheer indifference, are throwing grit into the machine of demobilisation' (13 December); 'Hundreds of thousands of men are not wanted at the front but are badly needed at home' (18 December); 'It is not the privates, it is the generals who are the trouble. The military authorities are like the Pharaohs of old: they harden their hearts and will not let the people go' (20 December);

> Will nothing bring home to the Government the seriousness of the immediate need for demobilisation? . . . The *Daily Express* does not believe that the Government realises the depth of hostile feeling that has been raised among all classes, and particularly among the fighting men, by all this deplorable delay [28 December].

Then, after Lloyd George's crushing election victory announced on that day:

> We trust the Government will not think that their colossal majority entitles them to disregard public opinion . . . What is wrong with demobilisation? It may be sheer indifference on the part of those in power, or it may be a complicated red-tape bungle, or it may be a refusal by the military to release the soldiers [30 December].

All this was accompanied by a series of bitter cartoons, showing soldiers on a quayside, tied to it by 'red tape'; or tied to a tree like the heroine in the ancient fable; or sitting in a circle outside the Demobilisation Office, singing: 'It may be for years, and it may be for ever'; or a soldier on the quayside picking the petals off a flower – 'This year, next year, sometime, never' – while an American transport moves away to sea.

But, throughout, the *Daily Express* did not hesitate to point to the reasons which could explain to any intelligent soldier, as well as to the mass of its readers, why 'the generals' might be interested in delay. 'We are not concerned with Russia,' another editorial ran on 18 December:

> We are not concerned with the Estonians or the Finns. Curious delegates speaking for one faction of what once was Russia come to the Allies, and in particular to Great Britain, asking that they should interfere. They ask us to declare war on some Russians to befriend others . . . There is no reason why we should have war thrust upon us . . . We do not know of any reason that makes the affairs of Russia the concern of the British Empire.

On 3 January the paper came out with a big headline right across the front page: 'Are We to be Committed to a War with Russia?' Inside were two editorials. One was on demobilisation, directly attacking the highest military authorities, the Commander-in-Chief and the Chief of the Imperial General Staff:

> Have Sir Eric Geddes and his colleague Sir Robert Horne got the power to get men out, or are Sir Douglas Haig and Sir Henry Wilson in a position to block the whole road? If so, it is the plain duty of the War Cabinet to remove the obstruction.

Then followed a second editorial, headed 'Not Another War'. It said:

> There are ominous signs that the country, rejoicing over the peace it has so well won, is to be committed without a word said to another gigantic campaign. Some newspapers are already clamouring for a war to the death against the Bolshevists. Ships and missions are being moved in a disquieting fashion . . . The public, with whose bodies such a war would be fought, knows no more about the intentions of the Government than the man in the moon. It is said that we must recover the £350,000,000 we have lent to Russia. Such a bondholders' war would be indeed a bad investment. A six months' campaign with a million men would leave us in the end without our £350,000,000 and with an extra debt twice that size. Imagine the feelings of the man waiting for his demobilisation papers who is shipped off suddenly to Reval, or

Danzig or Odessa. Frankly, the country will not stand it. We are sorry for the Russians, but they must fight it out among themselves. Great Britain is already the policeman of half the world. It will not and cannot be policeman of all Europe. We want to return to industry and to repair the ravages of war. We want to see our sons home again. In fact, we want peace. The frozen plains of Eastern Europe are not worth the bones of a single British grenadier.

The very next day the paper rounded off this frontal attack on the British Government's war with a final denunciation – as immediately following events proved – in an editorial headed 'Withdraw From Russia'. Reverting to the probability that to occupy Moscow and Petrograd the Allies would send 1 million men, it said: 'Once you have landed your army, circumstances swallow the best-intentioned Governments as a boa-constrictor swallows a rabbit' – and it branded such a 'visionary' campaign as similar to the one 'which proved fatal to Napoleon'.

There can be no doubt – especially for any who, like the present writer, was serving in the British army at the time – that this crescendo of denunciation by a penny newspaper with a circulation approaching (at that time) 0.5 million had a far greater influence on the *mass reader* than, say, the campaign of *The Times*, the circulation of which was about a quarter of that figure, or the *Morning Post*, which sold far fewer copies. Both those papers, like the *Daily Telegraph*, which had a larger circulation than *The Times*, were not read by the working man, the small shopkeeper, or the ordinary soldier.

And on 3 January 1919 it was the ordinary soldier who took a hand in the debate.[17]

NOTES

1 War Cabinet papers in the Public Record Office: CAB. 23/4, Minute 289.
2 CAB. 23/8, WC 489.
3 CAB. 23/4, WC 494, 500, 505.
4 Ibid., WC 497.
5 C. E. Calwell, *The Life of Sir Henry Wilson* (London: 1927) p. 148.
6 Quoted by M. Gilbert, *Winston S. Churchill*, IV (London: 1975) p. 226.
7 CAB. 23/4, WC 502.
8 Quoted by Gilbert, op. cit., p. 226.

9 CAB. 23/4, WC 511.
10 Calwell, op. cit., p. 155.
11 Lloyd George, *The Truth About the Peace Treaties*, I (London: 1938) pp. 327–8.
12 WO 33, 957; GT 6434.
13 Calwell, op. cit., p. 155.
14 WO 32, 5242 under 1 January 1919.
15 WO 162, 14. p. 18.
16 *Istoricheski Arhiv* (Moscow, 1961) no. 6. p. 68. The 'generously financed' propaganda from outside was, of course, a myth: Soviet Russia was completely cut off from Europe at the time, in an encirclement of enemy armies and navies, and no such 'generous finance' could possibly get through.
17 Out of nearly fifty cases of soldiers' and sailors' action described in Chapter 3 of this book, a few have been mentioned earlier. The *Annual Register* (1919) listed those at Folkestone, Dover, Osterley Park, Kempton Park and Brighton, without details. The first four, in some detail, were described by T. H. Wintringham in his *Mutiny* (London: 1937), with eight others only listed. He reproduced, in all essentials, the story of the Calais strikes originally printed in *Workers' Life* (1929), but merely listed others at Dunkirk, Rosyth, Devonport and Port Edgar. Graham Wallace in *RAF Biggin Hill* (London: 1957) described the strike at that camp. G. Bennett also mentioned the sailors' strikes at Rosyth and Milford Haven (*Cowan's War*, London: 1964). A pamphlet, *Mutiny!* (*Spark*, Brighton, 1968), by A. Killick also gives no more than the 1929 account of Calais. Another pamphlet by David Lamb, published in 1978 (*Mutinies, 1917–1920*, Solidarity, London and Oxford), summarised most of these reports.

3 The Soldiers Intervene

FOLKESTONE AND DOVER

On Saturday morning, 4 January, there had been what *The Times* on 6 January described as 'a beautiful ceremony' at the Wellington Barracks in London, when three battalions of the Grenadier Guards, three battalions of the Coldstreams, two of the Scots Guards, and one each of the Irish and Welch Guards, saw off their respective detachments, under colours flying and with massed bands, in the presence of Queen Alexandra, Prince Olav of Norway and several thousands of spectators, on their way to Charing Cross Station. There the colour parties were to entrain on their way to Cologne. But at the last moment, after they had marched through the streets, their departure was countermanded – 'owing to the fact that it had been necessary to close *Folkestone* as the port of embarcation, in consequence of trouble among the troops returning to France from leave in England,' said *The Times* on its main news page.

What had happened? The story can be pieced together from the main account by the Folkestone correspondent of *The Times*, supplemented by those of the reporters of other newspapers. On the morning of Friday, 3 January 1919, notices were posted that 1000 men were to parade for embarcation at 8.15 a.m. and another 1000 at 8.25 a.m. The men wrote across them: 'No men to parade'.[1] Word was passed along from rest camp to rest camp that the men in one, nearly 3000 of them, had held a meeting and had decided not to march down to the boat, but to visit the Mayor of Folkestone.[2] Shortly after 9 a.m. a large body of men from No. 1 Rest Camp marched in orderly fashion to No. 3 Rest Camp at the other end of the town. There the column was heavily reinforced, and all marched down the Sandgate Road to the town hall. On the way they shouted in chorus: 'Are we going to France?' and answered with a louder 'No!' Then: 'Are we going home?' – and in response a resounding 'Yes!'[3] Over 10,000 men in all assembled at the town hall. Several climbed on to its portico and delivered speeches: their complaints that many applications for demobilisation, in order to return to waiting jobs, were being ignored, were greeted with cheers.[4] The mayor told the men that if they went back to camp they would hear good news: a remark answered by the singing of 'Tell Me the Old, Old Story'![5] During the demonstration at the town hall the soldiers saw an officer taking photographs from the window. They entered the building and demanded an interview with him. He turned out to be an Australian taking the pictures as a souvenir, and offered the film to the soldiers – which they accepted.[6] Finally the town commandant, Lieutenant-Commander H. E. J. Mill, promised the men that 'any complaints would be listened to': and they then returned to their camps in a long procession, preceded by a big drum. At the camps they were told (1) that the pivotal and slip men who had work to go to could, if they wished, be demobilised at once, from Folkestone; (2) that those who had any complaints could have seven days' leave in order to pursue their case; and (3) that those who wished to return to France could do so. 'They seemed reassured,' reported *The Times* Correspondent, who underlined that there had been 'no rowdyism'.[7] He said that later a number of the men did return to France: however, the *Daily News* correspondent wrote that the morning mail boat to France had sailed without any troops.

On Saturday morning, 4 January, there was a new demonstration. Despite the assurances given the previous day, 'a certain number' had been ordered to France that morning. They refused, and a large number marched to the harbour to station pickets there, while other pickets were posted at the station, meeting the trains with men returning from leave: all joined the strike. Only officers and overseas troops embarked on the boats for Boulogne, which left 'practically empty'.[8] According to the *Morning Post* correspondent, an armed guard had been mounted at the harbour,

> whereupon a representative of the soldiers threatened that, if it remained, they would procure their arms from their quarters at the rest camp and forcibly remove the guard. The latter was consequently withdrawn, and the malcontents placed pickets at the approaches to the harbour to prevent British soldiers from entering. Dominion soldiers were however allowed to go.[9]

Probably about the same incident, a *Herald* investigator several days later said that the guard consisted of Fusiliers with fixed bayonets and ball cartridges. When the pickets approached, one rifle went up: 'the foremost picket seized it, and forthwith the rest of the picket fell back'. Everywhere the feeling was the same, he said: 'The war is over, we won't fight in Russia, we mean to go home.'[10]

The same reporter stated that the soldiers also tore down a large label, 'For Officers Only', above the door of a comfortable waiting-room. *The Times* report went on to say that several thousand men, including the new arrivals carrying their kits and rifles, marched to the town hall, where they were once again addressed by their spokesmen. It was announced that a 'Soldiers' Union' had been formed, and that it had elected a committee of nine to confer with the authorities in the town hall. There would be, immediately afterwards, a meeting with the general and the town commandant at No. 3 Rest Camp. The whole mass of about 10,000 men marched there to await the report of the conference, which lasted into the afternoon. Finally the delegation announced to the soldiers that the pledges made the previous day had been renewed. Late that evening, in fact, special staff from the Ministry of Labour arrived, and went to each rest camp to complete the necessary formalities.

Once more the correspondent remarked that there had been 'no rowdiness', and that the townspeople spoke 'in the highest possible terms' of the soldiers' behaviour.[11] Thereafter everything proceeded as had been agreed.

It is not without interest that, as it turned out, one of the nine delegates was a solicitor in civil life, and another a magistrate.[12] The composition of the delegation was: one sergeant of the Army Service Corps (chairman), a corporal of the Royal Engineers, a gunner of the Royal Garrison Artillery, and the rest privates, several of whom were trade unionists.[13]

After this unprecedented action at *Folkestone*, another took place at *Dover* on Saturday, 4 January. About 2000 men took part, holding a meeting near the Harbour Station, at which a deputation was elected to see the military and civil authorities.[14] The *Daily Chronicle* report gave further details:

A number of men had reached the Admiralty Pier, where transports were waiting for them, when suddenly there was a movement back, and men began to leave the pier. They streamed off along the railway, in spite of official protests, and on their way to the town met a train loaded with returning troops bound for the pier. The soldiers called on the newcomers to join them, and the carriages were soon emptied. Continuing their march, and all in full field kit and carrying their rifles, the troops mustered at Cresswell, and from the railway bridge some of their number addressed the others on demobilisation grievances. They decided to send a deputation to the military and civil authorities, and the men then fell in and marched to the Town Hall, which was reached just before 10 o'clock . . . The troops represented scores of different units, and a number of Canadian and Australian men.[15]

At the town hall, they formed up on either side of the road and in the side streets. The Mayor admitted them into the town hall, and the overflow into the adjoining Connaught Hall. While waiting for a reply from the military authorities, the men sang popular songs, and the Mayor arranged for their free admission to the cinema. In the afternoon, at the town hall, they received promises that grievances would be 'looked into', and returned to their rest camps.[16] A War Office statement printed by *The Times* said that the soldiers' representatives were seen first by General Dallas, GOC Canterbury, and then by General Woolcombe, head of the Eastern Command. He had returned from leave when hearing of the 'trouble', and from Folkestone had telephoned the Home Army Command at the War Office for instructions. The assurances he gave were on the same lines as at Folkestone. A report in *The Times* next day stated that 'all cases had been enquired into', and that soldiers were being allowed freely to telegraph their employers: if the latter replied favourably, the men could go home to start work at once.

MORE IN KENT

Late on Friday, 3 January, the London evening papers had printed brief accounts of what was happening at Folkestone: which of course had become known at Dover. But almost immediately, in the words of the *Evening News* the following Monday, 'the censorship came into action, with the result that all authentic news was stopped' (though the *Star*, on Saturday, 4 January, defied the ban). There can be no doubt about the military authorities' reaction. The London letter in the Plymouth *Western Morning News* on 6 January, referred to 'someone's desire to conceal the truth: an attempt had been made on Friday and Saturday to hide the trouble at Folkestone . . . despite the efforts of the War Office to conceal it, nearly 10,000 men took extreme action'. The *Birmingham Gazette* on 8 January confirmed that 'when the Folkestone trouble first arose, the War Office invoked what is left of the censorship system to keep the whole matter out of the newspapers'. And on the same day *The Times*, evidently more directly accessible to War Office pressure than the provincial press, revealed another aspect of the events by now occurring in many places when it stated in its leading article:

> We are asked to publish, but have no intention of publishing, a great many letters on the subject of demobilisation which show a deplorable lack of responsibility on the part of the writers . . . fanning an agitation which is already mischievous and may become dangerous . . . These demonstrations by soldiers have gone far enough.

Later it will be shown that these angry words reflected real alarm in official quarters.

But *The Times* was too late. The demonstrations had certainly spread far beyond Folkestone, thanks to the reports in Friday's evening papers: *The Times* itself had to report, on Tuesday, 7 January, that the Folkestone and Dover demonstrations had been 'followed by similar protests in other parts of the country', and there might be more that day.

At other camps in Kent the demonstrations had already begun. At *Shortlands, near Bromley*, where there was a depot of 1500 men of the Army Service Corps, a committee of twenty-eight had been formed at breakfast on 6 January, including five NCOs and three cadets. Their chairman was a private from Canada, who had been at the front and had been transferred to the ASC.[17] They marched in column to Bromley, where they held a meeting in the Central Hall. The chairman stated their main grievances: delay in demobilisation, and being held in the army to do civilian work. During the meeting a message arrived from the camp, saying that there would be no more drafts overseas, those men already out on a convoy would be sent back to the depot, and demobilisation would start on Wednesday, 8 January.[18] On their return, the commanding officer asked for the names of the 'ringleaders': but this was refused,[19] and next morning he had a two-hour meeting with the committee. Apart from the promises already made, he agreed to send to the War Office a 'points system' of priorities for demobilisation which the committee had drawn up. This provided: married men with work to go to, and those running a one-man business – 1 point; years of service to be additionally credited as follows: 1914 4 points, 1915 3 points, 1916 2 points, 1917 1 point; men over military age, 1 additional point; those transferred from the infantry, 1 additional point. It appointed a sub-committee of five to visit other ASC depots in the London area. Meetings similar to their own had already been held at *Grove Park* and *Sydenham* on 6 January.[20] On 8 January the committee issued a statement that all the other ASC depots had approved the scheme, but with 2 points instead of 1 for men with one-man businesses.[21] Two days later demobilisation began.

At *Maidstone*, on 7 January, a demonstration of several hundred soldiers of the Queens, 3rd Gloucestershire and 3rd Wiltshire Regiments, marched down the High Street at 10 a. m., and held a meeting explaining their grievances. Thence they marched to the town hall, where the mayor received a deputation from them and promised to forward their representations to the proper quarters.[22] The demonstration had been preceded by interviews with their officers, at which the soldiers had demanded an end to unnecessary guard duties, drill and fatigues. During the afternoon demonstrations it became known that these demands had been conceded.[23] The demonstrations had been renewed by 600–700 men of all three regiments.[24]

At *Biggin Hill, Westerham*, on 7 January, some 700 men working on aeroplanes and wireless instruments refused to go on parade, and took possession of the camp. All its sections were placed under guard except for the officers' quarters. They got ready twenty-eight motor wagons for a journey to Whitehall. They were persuaded not to see the plan through by the 'tactful speech' of their former colonel, who addressed them in a large hangar. The next day (8 January) he promised his help if they put their grievances in writing. This they did, complaining of (1) insufficient food, badly cooked; (2) indescribable sanitary conditions, with eight washbasins for 700 men; (3) exploitation by the officers, who required the men to do private jobs for them; and (4) delays in demobilisation. The ex-colonel offered to accompany a deputation to the War Office if required. On 9 January officials from the War Office visited the camp and made immediate improvements in the sanitary and working conditions. On 10 January all except thirty-four men were sent home on ten days' leave.[25] Meanwhile, on 8 January, a number of RAF lorry drivers had refused to convey the 200 civilian workers on the aerodrome from their houses in South-East London several miles away: this had been done previously by civilian drivers, and the RAF men now demanded pay for this work at civilian rates.[26] They resumed work on 11 January, after an investigation had been promised.[27]

At *Richborough* 'there was a demonstration by troops' on 8 January; but beyond this bare mention in Lloyd George's own paper, nothing so far had been found.[28]

THE LONDON REGION

Since it was from the London evening papers that the general public and the soldiers had had first news of the doings at Folkestone and Dover, it is not surprising that some events at least as dramatic took place around and in the capital.

At *Osterley Park* – a big manor house in its own grounds, west of London – at least 3000 men of the Army Service Corps were stationed. Most of them had served in France, and had been wounded, in the infantry; later they had been drafted into the ASC,[29] and nearly all were ex-drivers of London buses, many with long trade union experience. They had recently laid their grievances about demobilisation before their commanding officer, but had had no definite reply.[30] Accordingly, on Monday, 6 January, the soldiers broke camp, and about 150 took out three lorries and drove to Whitehall, intending to call on Lloyd George. They told reporters that more would have come with them, but officers had removed parts of the mechanism of other lorries. From Downing Street, where they were joined by men of other regiments, they went to the Demobilisation Department at Richmond Terrace, where a deputation of six was received by a staff officer of the Quartermaster-General's Department. He informed them that from Wednesday, 8 January, 200 a day would be demobilised, adding that their complaints could not be investigated unless they returned to camp. This they did, followed by several staff officers and Ministry of Labour officials in a car.[31] In the afternoon a second deputation of two privates came to Whitehall from a meeting of both ASC and other units.[32] The War Office later issued a statement to the meeting saying that a beginning had already been made with dispersals for the Army Ordinance Corps, the Army Service Corps, the Army Pay Corps and other military organisations.[33] Meanwhile, at the afternoon parade in Osterley, a staff major had also told the soldiers that the Army Council, in session on Saturday, 4 January, had decided to put the Army Service Corps on the same footing for demobilisation as other units, and that none of them would be sent on draft overseas.[34]

The special significance of the latter assurance is underlined by a statement in the evening *Pall Mall Gazette*, on the day of the demonstration, that 'the excitement among the Army Service Corps at Osterley and elsewhere is attributed in many quarters to oft-repeated rumours that plans are being prepared for the sending of a considerable force to Russia'.[35] In spite of the assurances received on this score, all training ceased on 7 January, and 100 men were told they were being demobilised immediately.[36] The demonstration of the others proceeded the following day.

At *Grove Park* (south-east of London), about 250 Army Service Corps drivers broke camp on 6 January and marched to the barracks half a mile away, asking to see the commanding officer. A sergeant-major who tried to stop them at the gates was knocked over in a scuffle, and the men entered. There they were 'met in a conciliatory spirit' by a senior officer, who, standing on a box, expressed sympathy with their grievances, and said everything in the officers' power was being done to secure their release. A spokesman of the men said that many of them had had letters from their employers offering them re-employment, but nothing had been done, and they were being kept in the army doing no useful work. At the commanding officer's request, they paraded again after dinner and filled in 'Form Z16' (for demobilisation).[37] Fifty men who had been ordered to go to Slough, three hours' journey by lorry, to scrub huts, refused, saying it was unreasonable to expect men to stand closely packed in lorries for such a period.[38]

At *Uxbridge* (North-West London), on Monday, 6 January, 400 men from the Armament School (used as a demolition centre) broke camp at midday and marched along the High Street singing, 'Britons Never Shall Be Slaves' and 'Tell Me the Old, Old Story'. At the market place they held a meeting, where they were addressed by the commandant, and then marched back. One of them told a reporter that, apart from the slowness of demobilisation, 'the food had been rotten since the Armistice, 1 loaf between 8 men, 5 days a week sausage'. That morning the men had upset the tables, and gone out. On their return they formed a Messing Committee composed of 4 or 5 privates, 1 sergeant and 1 officer. Not satisfied, on Tuesday, 7 January, they set up a Grievance Committee in each squad, composed of officers as well as men, to bring forward their complaints to the commandant. They also sent a deputation by lorry to the War Office.[39]

From *Kempton Park* (south-west of London), on Tuesday, 7 January, shortly before 3 p.m., thirteen large army lorries drove to the War Office in London, with forty to fifty soldiers in each lorry. General Burns had visited the depot that morning, but had not been able to give them any satisfaction. All were in high spirits, 'determined to get what they called their rights'. On the lorries they had chalked: 'No red tape', 'We want fair play', 'We're fed up', 'No more sausage and rabbits', 'Kempton is on strike'. Held up at the Horse Guards (the War Office), they elected a deputation of eleven, which went into the War Office 'amid ringing cheers'.[40] The result of the interview was not published, but it could not have differed from what was secured elsewhere.

At *Fairlop naval aerodrome* (near Ilford, east of London), orders were posted on the morning of 7 January that eighty men were to proceed to other camps. All 400 men paraded and asked for a conference with the commanding officer, Colonel Ward: the transport men meanwhile got out their lorries to go to Whitehall, should the interview prove unsatisfactory. The colonel, however, came to a mass meeting held in a hangar, and agreed that every man with papers showing he had employment to go to, or who came from a one-man business, should have a day's leave immediately, to get the papers endorsed, and could then go home pending demobilisation.[41]

At the *White City* (well within the boundaries of West London itself), about 100 Army Ordnance Corps men on 7 January refused to leave barracks for the 1.30 p.m. parade, and sent a deputation to one of the officers demanding (1) speedy demobilisation, (2) shorter working hours, (3) no church parades on Sunday, and (4) weekend passes when not on duty. They asked for a definite answer within a week, and meanwhile resumed duty.[42]

In the *Upper Norwood* camp (in South-East London), there was a distribution centre for men discharged from hospital after lengthy illness. 'After many previous discussions among themselves', they sent a deputation on Sunday, 5 January, to interview the commandant. Then, on 6 January, they discussed with him complaints raised by the men, chiefly that, even after twenty-eight days in hospital, they were not being discharged.[43]

But the most impressive demonstration of all, in the London region, was that at *Park Royal* (in North-West London) on 7 January, where there were 4000 men of the Army Service Corps. That day a committee elected by the soldiers submitted to their commanding officer the following demands: (1) speedier demobilisation; (2) reveille to be sounded at 6.30 in the morning, not 5.30; (3) work to finish at 4.30 in the afternoon, not 5.30; (4) no men over forty-one to be sent overseas; (5) all training to stop; (6) a large reduction of guard and picket duty; (7) no compulsory church parade; (8) no drafts for Russia; (9) a committee of one NCO and two privates to control messing arrangements for each company; (10) a written guarantee of no victimisation. Most of these demands were agreed to.[44]

However, at 1 p.m. on 8 January a big deputation arrived at Whitehall to present their demands themselves. This had been agreed to by the committee: they left volunteers behind to look after the 300 horses at the depot.[45] Their intention was to see the Prime Minister.

At Paddington, and again at the Horse Guards parade ground, they were met by General Feilding, commanding the London district, who tried to stop them, even threatening to use the police against them. Feilding promised them that demobilisation would take place 'as soon as possible': but as regards the assurance which they wanted that 'they would not be sent to Russia', he could give them none. This failed to satisfy them; they defied him, and marched in a body to Downing Street.[46] Apparently the general told them 'they were soldiers, and would have to obey orders'.[47]

Finally General Sir William Robertson, former Chief of the Imperial General Staff, came out to speak to them and hear their demands. He agreed that the commanding officer of the Home Forces should receive a deputation of one corporal, one lance-corporal and one private for half an hour. The deputation returned with a group of officers, who announced that the outcome of the talk was satisfactory, and Sir William Robertson had promised to send a general to Park Royal to investigate their complaints. While all this was going on, crowds of the general public were watching the proceedings and encouraging the men. One of the officers invited the men to go back to camp. But they insisted that first of all they

THE SOLDIERS INTERVENE   47

must hear a report from the deputation itself. Two or three of its members spoke. They confirmed that the same percentage of men at Park Royal would be demobilised as elsewhere: no one who had been overseas or was over forty-one would be sent on draft – 'including to Russia', added the *Daily Telegraph* reporter – and those already notified for draft were to be sent on Christmas leave, if they had not been sent already.

On their return, the men held a meeting in the canteen and expressed their satisfaction at the settlement.

Among the demonstrators at the War Office on 6 January were 250 soldiers due to return from leave to Salonika. They were nearly all time-expired men who had served in Greece (some for as long as three years) and before that in India. They were addressed by the Assistant Secretary for Demobilisation, General de Saumarez, who told them that those with demobilisation papers already prepared would be discharged immediately, and the remainder could go to the reserve battalions at home. If they could get their employers to send them the necessary form requesting their discharge, they too would be demobilised at once. Next morning, Thursday, 9 January, after assembling at the War Office again, they were marched to Chelsea Barracks, and there either demobilised or sent on fourteen days' leave for the purpose indicated.[48]

SUSSEX

An important demonstration took place at a great camp for convalescent soldiers at *Shoreham*, five miles along the seafront from Brighton. Between 7000 and 8000 men participated.

At Lewes (the county centre), on Sunday evening, soldiers had asked all civilians to leave the local cinema so that they could hold a meeting. This was agreed, and in the hall, packed to overflowing, several speakers addressed them. They agreed to meet at Shoreham next morning. When they did so, the commanding officer at Shoreham tried to dissuade them.[49] He told them that nothing could be done for six to eight weeks, but they would not listen. Many wore decorations and wound stripes.[50] A local reporter wrote of 'the measured tramp of a marching column, in regular regimental formations, but without officers, bugles or drums' (singing and waving Union Jacks, said *The Times*). Throughout Sunday, 5 January, the men's leaders had been busy collecting promises of support from the troops for a march out of camp next day: they assembled on parade at 7 a.m. on the Monday. 'The Brigadier-General addressed them and promised to forward their grievances, offering to meet them again later: but the leaders of the men decided to march at once to Brighton.' At *Southwick* they were joined by Royal Marine Engineers, 'and on the way into Brighton every soldier in the streets was invited to join in the procession. One of the leaders, wearing two wound stripes, told the reporter about the hardships they were meeting, particularly wasting time when they could be working. The same man, in his speech at the town hall, amid cheers emphasised that they were there on behalf not only of men in the camp, 'but also of their less fortunate comrades still in France'.[51]

A deputation was received by the mayor, who then addressed the 'vast throng', promising to telephone the War Office, and to press the War Cabinet with the request that all in the camps should be sent home pending demobilisation. He agreed that they had grievances, that there were too many delays in demobilisation, but 'it was a very big job'. He informed them that a hot dinner was waiting for them on their return, and that there was no question of punishment. In fact, at a mass meeting on their return, the commanding officer of the district promised to send their views to the War Office without delay.[52] As he could not himself give any pledges, the men decided by a vote not to go on parade next day (i.e. Tuesday, 7 January), and to march to Worthing, where there were other camps.

The march was prevented by heavy rain, and the men decided instead to send a telegram to the Prime Minister, and meanwhile to resume normal duties. However, if there were no satisfaction within two days, they would resume the strike. In the meantime, they released one of their number who had been arrested. On 9 January the strike was resumed by men of the Royal Garrison Artillery; but the Prime Minister's message announcing the speed-up of demobilisation reached them the same day, and the strike was ended.[53]

The following is the text of the telegram they sent to Lloyd George:

> We men of the London Command Depot, Eastern Command Depot, 1st Siege Artillery Reserve Brigade and Training Wing, situated at Shoreham-by-the Sea, Sussex, bring to your notice the

following resolution: 'That we demand the instant demobilisation of all men here, by being sent home pending demobilisation papers being forwarded to us, thereby enabling us without delay to return to civil life'.[54]

HAMPSHIRE

In the afternoon of Tuesday, 7 January, several hundred men of the Army Service Corps, the Army Ordnance Corps and the Royal Engineers at *Aldershot* marched through their camp and came out into the town, where for half an hour they paraded the streets of this small garrison centre – the home for decades of military tradition and training. They went to the garrison headquarters, where a deputation interviewed the general commanding the garrison. He promised that their demand for demobilisation would receive consideration, whereupon they marched back to their barracks.[55] The local weekly newspaper, which did its best to belittle the significance of this 'minor demonstration', nevertheless admitted that 'in common with all other military centres, Aldershot during the past week has been experiencing some of the unrest exhibited by the troops anxiously awaiting demobilisation'.[56] What it did not mention was that 'here and there were cries: "Will they send us to Russia?"'[57]

In the upshot, three large detachments were demobilised on 8 January, with officials working day and night to get the necessary papers ready. Special trains were arranged to take the demobilised men away; and a Soldiers' Committee, consisting of 100 men from each of the three corps mentioned earlier, supervised the proceedings throughout.[58]

Winchester was one of the scenes of 'demonstrations of an orderly character . . . by large numbers of soldiers'. On Monday morning, 6 January, the troops of 'one unit in the Winchester district', numbering about 150, marched from their camp through the city to the barracks gate, and thence returned 'singing' to the Broadway, where a speech was made by one of their number 'on the subject of demobilisation, better feeding and less red tape'. An officer stated that the commanding officer would receive a deputation, and the troops returned to their quarters.[59]

On 7 January a soldiers' demonstration took place at *Longmoor Camp, East Liss*, but no further details seem to have been published.[60]

Much later, on 16 January, 400 men of the Royal Air Force marched from *Beaulieu Camp* to *Lymington*, where they set forth their demands to the mayor: men over forty-one to be demobilised at once, those under forty-one with their own businesses or employment waiting to be given leave pending general demobilisation, or, if they had no employment, to be given twenty-eight days' leave to find work. The mayor promised to forward their complaints to the Air Ministry.[61]

Here may be mentioned a very discreet report from the *Isle of Wight*, at the end of the first week in January: 'Some regrettable military incidents, from which even the Island has not been free, have taken place during the past week in connection with difficulties which have arisen over the demobilisation of the troops'.[62] Most of the local weeklies published on the island did not mention where the incidents occurred, obviously under pressure from the military censorship. But one did slip through the network:

> The dissatisfaction demonstrated at many camps throughout the country at the irritating methods of demobilisation have been reflected at Freshwater. Exceptional scenes are said to have taken place at Golden Hill fort on Monday [6 January], where the men failed to parade for duty. Resentment as to the cooking of the food, and especially at the spoiling of their Christmas dinner, has been felt for some time, and on Monday some spokesmen were put forward to state their complaints. It is said that these were put under arrest, and that the arrest led to the remainder of the battalion demanding their release and forcing the guard-room.[63]

According to the biographer of Lord Trenchard,[64] (using his private account dictated to a stenographer some years later and his official report to the War Office) Sir William Robertson in mid-January 1919 requested Trenchard (then Major-General) to go to *Southampton*, where the docks were in the hands of mutinous soldiers and '20,000 men were refusing to obey orders'. Trenchard found deserted troopships picketed by soldiers, and 5000 men in the customs shed. Shouted down and hustled by them, he secured 250 soldiers armed with rifles and ball ammunition, together with military police, from the Portsmouth garrison, intending 'to shoot if necessary'. This was contrary to explicit protests by the general in charge of the Southern Command. By marching his men into the customs shed and having them demonstratively load their rifles,

Trenchard secured the surrender of the 5000 and the arrest of 107 among them. By drenching 'about a hundred others' in their billets with ice-cold water from hose-pipes, he forced these, too, to line up submissively in blankets at his office. For this action, says the biographer, Trenchard was 'complimented' by Churchill.

The remarkable thing is that not one of the four contemporary Southampton papers gave the slightest hint of any strike, whether by 20,000 or by 5000 men. Neither did the *Annual Register* for 1919, published many months afterwards, although it did list seven other soldiers' strikes (pp. 5–6); nor did Churchill in his *Aftermath*, published in 1929, while also listing six strikes (pp. 54–62) – and he did not mention Trenchard at all in this connection, much less any compliments. The War Office papers available for scrutiny to the present writer in 1977 at the Public Record Office did not appear to include any report by Trenchard at all (though of course he might have kept a copy himself). As for the notes dictated to the stenographer, the biographer himself wrote that he found them, in his judgement, 'more reliable for expressions of opinion than for detailed facts such as dates, names of places and people, etc.'

None of the foregoing, however, rules out the possibility that a strike of 5000 soldiers did occur at Southampton (though in fact it would have been smaller than those at Folkestone or elsewhere). In that event, it would appear that the authorities, and Churchill himself, must have taken exceptional precautions to suppress any public mention of the whole event. This would not be surprising. *No such repressive action against soldiers as that described by Trenchard took place anywhere else in the British Isles, so far as can be ascertained.* Had any publicity been given to it at that disturbed time, whether in the press or in the House of Commons, the results would most probably have been very different from those which Trenchard considered he had obtained.

THE WEST COUNTRY AND WALES

At *Bristol*, on 7 January, 100 men of the 12th Battalion, Bedfordshire Regiment, marched from their depot to the Council House to ask help from the Lord Mayor in hastening their demobilisation. A deputation of three interviewed him and the representative of the Ministry of Labour. They objected to having to work at the docks, i.e. to doing civilian work at soldiers' pay. The Lord Mayor promised to forward their grievances to 'the proper quarters'.⁶⁵ However, on Saturday, 11 January, a further demonstration was held: 700 soldier mechanics of the Royal Air Force and Army Service Corps – 'really mechanics in khaki', as *The Times* reporter put it – marched from the Western Aircraft Depot at Yate to Bristol. They complained to the County Director of Demobilisation that men with long service in the forces were being retained while men who had recently joined were being released.⁶⁶ They were told – probably not entirely to their satisfaction – that the latter were either 'pivotal men' (on whom factories depended) or apprentices.⁶⁷ However, by then far-reaching demobilisation measures had begun.

At *Milford Haven* on a patrol vessel, HMS Kilbride, there took place on 13 January a 'mutiny not accompanied by violence'. The men were told to do two watches, but refused to do so for the pay they were receiving. They asked to see the captain, but this was refused: in reply, they refused to go to sea. The captain went ashore to report the matter, whereupon they hauled down the naval flag and hoisted the Red Flag. At a naval court-martial held in Devonport, the captain denied any ill-treatment or abuse of the men: the men, on the contrary, accused the temporary lieutenant who had been in command of abusing them, using the words that 'in the merchant service he had broken the hearts of niggers, and he would do the same with them'. The leading seaman on trial was acquitted; of the 7 sailors, 1 was sentenced to two years' hard labour, 3 to one year, and 3 to ninety days' detention.

This case, illustrating the more rigid spirit dominating the navy at the time, nevertheless was at bottom a vivid indication of the feelings of the lower deck. It was timely appreciation of those feelings which prompted the action of the Admiralty mentioned below.

'Among practically all the units in Plymouth Garrison,' wrote a local paper on 9 January, in a rare anticipation of events – or rather, admission of facts which were common knowledge, but which most newspapers up till then were afraid to print –

> there are a good many men who would welcome a speeding-up of the demobilisation arrangements. In some corps the slowness of procedure is merely regretted, in others, it is the cause of considerable dissatisfaction . . . On the whole, the men are content to let matters rest for the present, believing that the trouble at Dover and elsewhere will hurry the authorities.⁶⁸

However, this soothing assurance was misleading. On 7 January – the direct result of the previous weekend's demonstrations – it had been announced that the Admiralty had appointed a committee to meet representatives of the lower deck on questions of service pay and conditions.[69] With the sanction of the commander-in-chief, meetings of naval ratings were held in the Royal Naval Barracks, *Devonport*, to discuss 'questions of interest'. On 9 January, delegates from all branches of the lower deck on various ships met and adopted a resolution to 'act unitedly' in dealing with the Admiralty committee.[70] These delegates, about sixty in number, instructed their president, Alfred J. Lock, to send a letter to the Prime Minister, headed 'Royal Naval Barracks, Devonport, 10 January 1919, on behalf of the mass meeting of delegates of different classes, representative of lower deck ratings, held at Devonport on 9 January 1919, to consider ways and means of the best and loyal methods of presenting their grievances for better pay and conditions of service in the Royal Navy'. They had instructed him, 'unanimous in the hope that immediate steps will be taken to put this resolution into effect', to present Lloyd George with the following resolution: 'In view of the persistent and determined unsympathetic attitude of Dr Macnamara' [Parliamentary Secretary to the Admiralty] 'towards the petty officers and men of the Royal Navy, the Prime Minister is requested to relieve him of his duties forthwith.'[71]

This resolution, without precedent in its substance, was also unprecedented in the fact that it was communicated at once to the press – a procedure as effective as a strike would have been.

At *Falmouth*, the following event was recorded by the local paper:

[On Tuesday, 7 January] there was an exciting incident at Trevethan Camp, where the 25th Battalion Rifle Brigade are stationed. The trouble, it is stated, has arisen because the men as they alleged are drilled for what they consider too long, with night manoeuvres as well, up to war standard. This has engendered an ill-feeling which culminated on Tuesday in the whole battalion, 600 strong, refusing to parade in the afternoon. A call was made for the colonel, but he did not appear. The men then elected two spokesmen – one overseas and one home service man – to interview the C.O., the result being a promise that things would be put right. The men were afterwards dismissed. It is understood that the grievance has now been put right.[72]

The press in *Wales* gave practically no news of local protests by soldiers, except for a sentence that '*Newport* Town Hall was crowded yesterday by miner-soldiers who attended in connection with the scheme for release of men from the forces'.[73] At *Swansea* an editorial in the local daily newspaper asserted: 'Swansea was seething with complaints and misunderstandings, concerning the difficulties and delays connected with demobilisation, before troubles were reported as arising elsewhere.' Whether anything similar occured in this centre of the anthracite coal industry is not recorded: but significantly the same issue printed on its front page a report of the Western District of the South Wales Miners' Federation's meeting there on 4 January: 'A strong resolution was passed protesting against Britain interfering in the internal affairs of Russia and [demanding] that all British troops now in Russia should be withdrawn immediately.'[74]

SALISBURY PLAIN

The writer was a witness and participant in the events described in this section, and consequently it will be more natural to speak in the first person.

Ten days or so after the Armistice I was transferred from a cyclist (Yeomanry) regiment in Ireland to a newly formed unit – the Meteorological Section of the Royal Engineers, stationed at a big school of aerial navigation on Salisbury Plain. I knew nothing whatsoever about meteorology – nor, with one exception, did any others among more than 100 soldiers transferred at the same time, from the most varied military units all over Britain. The only thing common to all of us appeared to be that we had had a secondary education, while a few were teachers or university students (not as a rule in science faculties) in civil life. However, none of us had pursued any 'intellectual' occupation in the army, and I personally was a lance-corporal engaged in ordinary training of new recruits. There was accordingly much guessing, and not a little strong language, about such a transfer after the war was over.

The mystery was soon solved. One afternoon early in December – we had had only about ten days' training in our new 'profession' – company orders informed us that a staff major from the War Office would address the unit next day, to invite volunteers for the North Russian Expeditionary Force, who would work as specialists with the Royal Air Force. This caused, as far as I personally was concerned, a 'crisis of conscience', since in the spring of 1917 I had joined the British Socialist Party, which had later been consistently supporting the Bolsheviks and denouncing intervention. However, there was nothing for it: I was twenty years old, and felt I must face the music – although I had never spoken in public in my life.

That evening, with considerable trepidation (and after consulting only one friend), I got up in the crowded recreation room, asked for attention, and spoke on the subject of the next morning's parade. In outline, I tried to explain why the Russian people had overthrown the Tsar, what Lenin's government was doing, why the workers and peasants were supporting the Red Army and not the Whites, and why – irrespective of my political opinions, which probably they did not share – we should refuse to interfere with the efforts of the Russians to settle their own affairs: not forgetting to allude to what the English did with Charles I in 1649.

There was a moment's silence. Then the only NCO senior to me – a corporal with two wound stripes – said without rising: 'Well, Corporal Rothstein, I think you needn't worry about any of us volunteering. We've all had enough of this bloody war and this bloody army.' There was a hubbub of approval, and the ordeal was over – with a number coming over afterwards to slap me on the back. Only one, a boy of eighteen, took me aside and asked me to understand his position. He had been training as a professional meteorologist before he was called up, and his future career might depend on his getting this experience. All I could do was to remind him that, if he did go to north Russia, he might be abruptly deprived of any career at all . . .

Next morning we were duly paraded, and the man from the War Office, resplendent in gold braid and red tabs, addressed us on the horrors of Bolshevism and the great merits of going to Archangel – not forgetting that (whereas private soldiers' pay just then was 15*s. a week*, with a similar amount of 'separation allowance' for the family) the pay in North Russia would be 24*s. a day*, with a corresponding separation allowance. Then our commanding officer asked those willing to volunteer to step forward two paces – and only one, our young meteorologist, did so. It was a complete victory, and I have rarely seen a man more thunderstruck than the purple-faced major.

However, this was only the first part of the story. About a week after this incident, most of us were given 'extended ACI leave' for Christmas, like practically half the army stationed in Britain: and I rejoined my family with the certainty, for the first time since 1916, that when I came back on 2 January 1919, the end of military service would be in sight. However, on Christmas Eve a telegram arrived: 'Return to unit immediately' – and when I did so, it was to find that, with six others, also recalled from leave for the pleasures of Christmas in the army, I was on *compulsory draft* for Archangel! This device of compelling those who would not 'volunteer' was being widely practised.

For the moment, nothing could be done. We handed in our 'home army' equipment, and were issued with pistols, lanyards for the shoulder straps, emergency first aid equipment to sew into our greatcoats: we were given gas-masks of an improved pattern on 30 December, and passed through two new types of gas. In short, all preparations were made – as in so many other units of the army.

Then came the events at Folkestone and Dover, of which we had the first fragmentary news on Saturday, 4 January, based on the London evening papers' accounts the previous day. Late that night belated men 'on pass', returning from the great permanent camp at Larkhill – on a long ridge about 1½ miles away, across a gently sloping grassy valley – which accommodated thousands of men, reported that 'the Australians had broken loose', and were 'smashing everything up'. Next morning there was a smell of smoke in the air when we came out of our army huts, and over Larkhill wreaths of smoke were rising. Then the civilian milkman came round – a regular purveyor of news to units stationed in Britain – and reported that the garrison theatre at Larkhill had been set on fire by the 'Colonial' (now known as 'Dominion') troops: it had long been obnoxious to them because it was reserved for officers and warrant officers.

Within the next twenty-four hours, almost every aerodrome on the vast Salisbury Plain had its elected committee, or was preparing to elect one. In our unit that Sunday morning, I assembled our little draft and proposed to them that, as a junior non-commissioned officer, I should ask to see our commanding officer on their behalf the next morning. I would tell him that we had all, in December, refused to volunteer for north Russia, and resented very much now finding ourselves on compulsory draft. We regarded the war there as undeclared and illegal, and contrary to our undertakings on enlistment ('for three years or the duration of the war', whichever came first). I would request him accordingly either to give me an undertaking about immediate demobilisation, or – as Army

Regulations permitted – to take me before the general commanding the district, to whom I would wish to make a complaint. Naturally, my colleagues warmly approved.

Next morning, (Monday, 6 January) I duly came before the commanding officer and told him what we had agreed. In reality, he was in civilian life a meteorological scientist. He replied himself – and the words are engraved on my memory –

> Please tell the draft, Corporal Rothstein, that I quite understand their unwillingness to go to Russia. Tell them that all of us want to go back to civil life as soon as possible. As a matter of fact – but this is for your information only – we have just had a signal that demobilisation is to start on Friday [i.e. 10 January].

I thanked him, and hurried back to where the draft was waiting. Sure enough, a large batch were sent away to the hastily improvised discharge depot at the Crystal Palace (in South London) on 10 January, and I left with most of the remainder a few days later.

This, of course, was but one little corner of the ferment which was going on, all that week and the next, in the British armed forces. But two particular features may be noted.

The first is that the sensational events at Larkhill were completely hushed up by the press, of course under constraint from the military censors – although thousands of men knew of them. The nearest, very discreet, allusion was made by the editorial in a local paper the following weekend:

> It is deeply significant that the Government, contemporaneously with concessions in regard to liberating men, has now intimated that it is not the intention to send any more of our troops to Russia . . . Late events have enlightened the Government on the mind of the soldier as the arguments of their political opponents never did . . . Demobilisation was left to take care of itself, with the results we have just seen.[75]

The other is an entry in the historical record for 1919 of the War Office Headquarters Directorate of Organisation, kept at the Public Record Office:

> In October 1918 a demand was received for personnel for 2 Meteorological Sections [for the North Russian Relief Force]. 1

officer and 15 other ranks were prepared for embarcation, but ultimately 1 officer (Lieut. Pick) and 2 other ranks, all obtained from France, were sent.[76]

There is an odd parallel to the attempt in my unit in December 1918 to secure volunteers for north Russia and to the soldiers' reaction, although it may well have been on some (unnamed) aerodrome elsewhere:

> Demobilisation is the only topic of the conversation at all hours . . . But today the sergeant-major entered the dining-room and put the tin hat on everyone's feelings. With a solemnity befitting a solicitor reading the family will, he announced that volunteers were wanted for an expeditionary force to South Russia – Ye gods! Volunteers for Russia, when all that would satisfy the men was speedy demobilisation. Could a bigger joke be played by the authorities? Needless to say, the sergeant-major received no response, except a thunderous appeal for 'my ticket'.[77]

MIDDLE ENGLAND

Felixstowe (Suffolk). About 2000 Royal Air Force men and several thousand other soldiers demonstrated here on 8 January, protesting particularly against the retention in the army at this coastal home defence centre of men over forty-one.[78] The RAF men marched to the Defence headquarters at Harwich. They were received by Major-General Stanton, who promised to consider their grievances.[79]

Bedford. Two 'largely attended' soldiers' meetings (mainly Royal Engineers) were held at St Paul's Square, Bedford, on 4 and 5 January, after several thousand soldiers had marched through the town. Speakers called on the authorities to hasten the demobilisation of men 'at present engaged in trivial work'. Leaders of the demonstration were formed into a committee to put the soldiers' views to the area military authorities. On 5 January, the men had been addressed by Brigadier-General Fawcett, who explained the slowness of demobilisation by the fact that 'the war was not won yet, and *we still needed drafts for overseas, including Russia*' (my italics).[80] These explanations obviously did not satisfy the men: their representatives met the commanding officer on 6 January, and later reported the result at an evening meeting at Market Square. Once again it was found unsatisfactory. On 7 January four delegates were elected to meet the general again at 9 p.m. The next evening they reported back to another meeting at Market Square, that they had had over an hour's discussion with the general, who promised help in getting releases of pivotal and slip men and in other matters 'opposed to the War Cabinet's demobilisation system'.[81]

However, the same newspaper stated a fortnight later in its editorial that owing to continuing delays, 'discontent is inevitably rising again among the Engineers at Bedford . . . The last straw came this week, when a number of men who had been warned for departure [i.e. discharge] on Wednesday were informed that the arrangements were cancelled, and that they were not to go'. No details of how the discontent expressed itself were given. But a week later another editorial said that the Engineers had held a meeting in the drill hall, followed by a conference next day with an officer from the Eastern Command, who was 'duly impressed' – and after that demobilisation began in earnest.[82]

Kettering (Northamptonshire). On Thursday, 16 January, there was a short-lived strike of the Army Service Corps at the local Remounts Depot, prompted by a series of 'minor grievances'. After dinner all the men with the exception of two sergeants refused to return to the depot, and drew up a statement (1) complaining of the poor food, especially on night duty and of the attitude of a newly appointed officer; (2) pressing for three half-days 'off duty' a week; and (3) asking for an interval of three hours after coming off duty at 6 a.m. before going on duty again, instead of the fifteen minutes they were then getting.

A major failed to persuade the men to return to work, and the commanding officer, Colonel Tisdall, then spoke to them. He asked the men to make their complaints individually, whereupon the whole unit stepped forward. After this he heard them out sympathetically, agreed that their grievances were justified, and promised to put things right. At 4.30 p.m. the men, satisfied, returned to work.[83]

The contrast between official indifference (until events foreign to military regulations took place), the attempt to pursue strictly 'correct' methods of keeping soldiers in order, and the stubborn spirit of soldiers who felt – as everywhere in the army – that they were now 'civilians in khaki' and entitled to use civilian methods, could not be sharper.

Harlaxton (Lincolnshire). About 400 junior NCOs and men attached to the Royal Air Force at this little village near Grantham held a demonstration on 15 January on the question of demobilisation delays: they told a reporter that another 110 men on leave were 'in sympathy with their movement'. They marched to a field, where they elected a deputation which interviewed Wing-Commander Portal. Among other things, they asked (1) that all transfers (postings) to other stations – a frequent pretext for postponing demobilisation – should cease forthwith, except for men who had re-enlisted after discharge; (2) that men over forty-one, pivotal men, and those with employment awaiting them, should be immediately released or sent home on indefinite leave; and (3) that all parades should be cancelled.

When Portal came out to address the men, he told them that he had to send away miners and pivotal men first, but would try to accelerate other discharges, that he could not refuse postings, but would try to impress the higher authorities and that in general 'he was doing his best for them'. They marched back to camp to consider further action, and later on sent their leaders back to Portal. He gave them certain assurances, which the soldiers decided to accept – 'as satisfactory for the time being'.[84]

A remark by Winston Churchill in his volume on post-1918 affairs, *The Aftermath*, may mislead the reader. In his brief reference to the soldiers' protests against demobilisation delays, he wrote (p. 61) that 'the only serious rioting' was at *Luton, Bedfordshire*, where 'the Town Hall was burnt by the mob'. In reality, the rioting in question took place on Saturday and Sunday, 19 and 20 July 1919 – roughly six months after the soldiers' strikes described in this book. The very full accounts in the local newspapers (e.g. the *Bedfordshire and Hertfordshire Tuesday Telegraph*) from 22 July that year onward into August, including detailed police court reports, only mention one man in uniform – a Royal Marine – out of hundreds of local people who took part. Moreover, the cause of the outbreak, which took place during the weekend of celebrations of the Peace Treaty, was primarily dissatisfaction among ex-servicemen over pensions, and to some extent over the refusal of the Corporation to allow the ex-service organisations to hold their own commemoration service in a local park. While the affair certainly was one expression of the general atmosphere of political crisis existing in Britain in the summer of 1919, it has no place in the history of the soldiers' strikes at the beginning of that year.

THE NORTH

Leeds. An editorial in the *Leeds Mercury* on 7 January had already stated that 'those who mix with the soldiers know that serious discontent prevails among the troops at home either in the home camps or on leave'. One expression of this feeling on 10 January was a petition of the 700th Company (MT) of the Army Service Corps stationed in Leeds, stating that as the work of carrying munitions was ended, they should be demobilised. In the meantime, they wanted improvements in their rations and the abolition of Sunday church parades.[85]

This of course was not a strike, but under Army Regulations was no less a breach of discipline.

One of the rare 'war diaries' for infantry units which were kept up to the end of the war – or have survived the attentions of War Office 'weeders' – records an echo of the prevailing discontents at *Kilnsea*, near Spurn Head, Yorkshire. Here, on 9 January 1919, a detachment of the 3rd Reserve Battalion, King's Own Yorkshire Light Infantry, was working on Royal Engineers' fatigue work, digging cable trenches near the Blue Bell Inn. At 9 a.m., the record runs, the men refused to work owing to the waterlogged state of the trenches.

By 9.45 a.m. 'the disturbance was settled satisfactorily'. Again at 9 a.m., this time on 20 January, the men refused to march off to their working parties, owing to 'alleged' insufficiency of food. Again the 'disturbance' was satisfactorily settled in twenty minutes. This time the brigade major visited the station at 2 p.m. to investigate the 'disturbances' (eventually leaving four hours later).[86]

At *Heaton Park, Manchester*, on 9 January, 600 NCOs and men of the 562nd Home Employment Company went on strike and asked to see the colonel commandant, electing eight delegates for the purpose. The colonel received four of them. They complained that all of the men had served overseas, and a number were disabled: they were being held in the army, while men recruited more recently were being demobilised. They also complained of poor and insufficient food ('mainly biscuits during the past three weeks,' said one man). The colonel sent a special messenger to the War Office with a report.[87]

At *Blackpool*, there were 7000 men of the Royal Army Medical Corps. On Tuesday, 7 January, they held meetings in the morning and afternoon on the Promenade, and sent a petition to their colonel setting forth their demands. On Wednesday, 8 January, they held a mass meeting in Talbot Square in the evening, and then marched to the depot at the Coliseum. There some of the men were arrested, but their comrades broke the windows of the guardroom in a struggle to release them. On Thursday, 9 January, there was a general strike of the RAMC, who refused to go on any parade until their grievances had been settled. The colonel finally received a deputation 'sympathetically', promising (1) improvements in the food, (2) later hours (8 a.m.) for breakfast and (9 a.m.) for morning parade, (3) the abolition of squad and stretcher drill, and of the gas course, and (4) the end of compulsory church parades.[88]

On the evening of 10 January the men held an evening meeting at the Palace Theatre to hear the report of the deputation. In addition to the promises already made, the commanding officer said that 540 men a week would be demobilised.[89]

Naval men were involved in a movement at *Liverpool*. On Sunday, 12 January, 700 bluejackets paraded, led by their chief petty officers from the auxiliary warships. They demanded (1) immediate demobilisation, or indefinite leave pending demobilisation; (2) better food; (3) no swearing at them when giving orders; (4) 'to be treated as men, not as children by the officers'; and (5) no victimisation for taking part in the movement. The captain in command promised 'a remedy to all their grievances', congratulating the men on their 'orderliness'. On 13 January it was announced that 65 per cent were already being sent on leave pending demobilisation, and that all the other concessions requested had been granted.[90]

At *Holywood* (four miles from Belfast), men of the 3rd Somerset Regiment were very discontented at having to attend two parades daily, while demobilisation was being unnecessarily delayed. On Wednesday, 8 January, after reveille, the men assembled on the parade-ground in response to an 'unofficial' bugle call, and asked to see the colonel. He came out, and after hearing their complaint promised 'to do what he could'. The majority had served in France, many had been wounded. On Thursday, 9 January, it was announced that the second parade in the day had been cancelled. But a large number of the men marched to the Kinnegar firing range, stopped those who were firing and pulled up the flags and targets. Later, after being addressed by the general commanding the district, a number broke barracks and marched to Belfast.[91]

Royal Air Force men at *Cramlington* in *Northumberland* demonstrated on 9 January 'with a view to speeding up demobilisation at this station'. The general commanding 16th Group North-Eastern Area received their representatives. He told them that there was to be immediate demobilisation for (1) miners, (2) men over forty-one, (3) teachers and students, and (4) pivotal men, those with one-man businesses and those with employment contracts awaiting them. 'Satisfaction was expressed,' the newspapers reported.[92]

SCOTLAND

Edinburgh. About 100 men of the Highland Light Infantry marched on 8 January to the Scottish Command Headquarters. They had been brought from Haddington, East Lothian, four weeks before to be demobilised, but instead had been kept on guards, pickets, etc. All of them had served in France or in Mesopotamia. A deputation of four was received by the demobilisation officer, a major, to whom they set forth their grievances and their request for either immediate demobilisation or fourteen days' leave. He promised an investigation.[93]

Leith Fort. About 200 men of the Scottish Rifles, mostly transport workers, were being used on work in the docks. Most had served abroad in the war, and many were unfit for military service: but they were being kept on squad drill, while the food gave rise to repeated complaints. On Thursday, 9 January, they refused to drill, and had to be dismissed from parade.[94]

Stirling Castle. There was a 'disturbance' on Friday night, 10 January, in the 459th Agricultural Company, composed of soldiers employed on farming (as one of them told a reporter, 'We are lent out to farmers at low wages').[95] In addition they complained of delay in demobilisation. Two of them were arrested by the police for 'horseplay in the street', but their comrades stormed the police station and released them. A picket was sent by the military authorities to restore order. In court next morning one man was given two months' jail, another fined 40s.[96]

Rosyth. 'The discontent seething for fully a month almost boiled over last Friday [January 3] in the minesweeping flotillas with their base in the Firth of Forth', and the crews in some of them refused to go to sea.[97] Another account said that the discontent had been growing since the surrender of the German fleet. In the big battleships and cruisers discipline had been maintained, but it is unnecessary longer to conceal the fact that for more than a month the gravest trouble has existed among the auxiliary services, the crews drawn from the mercantile marine and trawlers, who have manned the innumerable patrol and minesweeping craft. Serious trouble occurred with the minesweepers based at Granton [on the Firth of Forth] – one of the chief minesweeping and patrol ports.

After the Armistice many of the men, who had served for four years, had demanded immediate demobilisation. The Admiralty had made several offers, which the men had refused, but on 3 January at Granton peace appears to have been restored by the offer of a bonus of £2 a week. 'Yesterday, however, said the *Dundee Courier* five days later, 'the men were saying "£100 to hazard your life every day for a year is not good enough", and many sailors refuse to put to sea'.[98]

The men were demanding that the Royal Navy should take over their duties, and that they should be allowed to get back to fishing. Finally, the Admiralty issued a statement on 8 January that only volunteers need go to sea.[99]

Cromarty. On the morning of 8 January, 700 men of the 3rd Reserve Battalion, Seaforth Highlanders, marched in a body from their camp in Cromarty. There one of their leaders, a private, addressed them, asking them to maintain order: they intended no disloyalty, and wanted only liberty and justice – but this demonstration was their only means of securing redress. Most of the men in the battalion had been wounded two or even three times. They sent a deputation to the general commanding the garrison of this northern base, who promised to meet them in camp. When the interview proved unsatisfactory, they decided on a further demonstration through the town, 'and a further resolution was passed' (text unpublished).[100] On 9 January all 700 refused to go on parade as a protest against the continued slowness of demobilisation. Interviews with their superior officers were not considered satisfactory, and another demonstration was held.[101]

It will not have escaped notice that some of the most significant incidents in Scotland, as in other parts of the United Kingdom, were not reported in the London press, and have had to be sought in the local newspapers, often weeklies. This of course was due to the continuing existence of military censorship and the general uncertainty about its powers. This uncertainty accounted not only for the sparseness of even the local newspapers' reports (that source may yet yield further examples of protest action), but also for the almost total silence of the Sunday newspapers of 5 January (twelve published in London and three in the provinces) about any soldiers' protests – even in Dover – apart from those at Folkestone.

OVERSEAS

In Great Britain, where the soldiers' strikes were taking place in the midst of a generally sympathetic population – and with a big strike movement extending rapidly among the industrial workers – the Government necessarily had to be very careful to avoid even a show of violence. Apart from the single naval incident at Milford Haven which was described earlier, nowhere were the soldiers' actions denounced either by the military authorities or by the press as 'mutinies' or even as 'insubordination': 'breaches of discipline' was the farthest that official language went.

Things were very different overseas, where protesting soldiers had no civilian support, and where it was comparatively easy to divide them by suppressing information on the one hand, and threatening to use force on the other. Nevertheless, the state of mind of the soldiers on the question of the devices being used to keep them in the army was no secret. It has been reflected discreetly even in some regimental histories written years afterwards, as the following examples will show:

> Unlike the French, who demobilised by classes, the British Government decided to draft men home by detachments according to the requirements of industry . . . Whatever the necessity for miners at home may have been, it certainly seemed unfair, and formed a very natural and reasonable grouse, for the men who had served throughout the war, that many of these miners returned to their civilian occupations after 3 months, and in some cases even less, in France. No other demobilisation was commenced until January 11 1919, but in the meantime orders, regulations and instructions had been flowing from all sources: numerous summaries and pamphlets from newspapers, speeches and orders were issued, giving information about demobilisation, and these were posted up for all ranks to read, and lectures on demobilisation were given by officers . . . It was extraordinary

how complicated it proved to be: the number of army forms which each man had to have filled up before he could leave was prodigious: the various interpretations of orders issued by every authority, from the War Office itself down to the battalion orderly-room, were so conflicting . . . Unfortunately no instructions were given with regard to length of service, age, etc., and, as in the case of miners, many very recently joined soldiers found themselves back in England, while many old soldiers were forced to remain in spite of guarantees of employment . . . On 21 December [1918] orders were received that men on leave could be demobilised, if their employers would guarantee them employment and their return was not essential for military reasons. This order naturally caused the greatest dissatisfaction and was cancelled on 8 January 1919 . . . The first large allotment for demobilisation came on January 11.[102]

Soon after Christmas, demobilisation was begun, with all its appalling complications of Forms Z, P, Q, and all the other letters of the alphabet . . . The first people to go home were all those who could claim any connection with a coal mine, and the last of these departed on January 1 1919.[103]

On December 30 we were given a lecture on the subject of demobilisation . . . After the lecture our feelings were rather mixed . . . Especially when we realised that presumably the length of one's service overseas was not to be taken as a just reason for priority in demobilisation. The promises we had previously received on this point were, in common with many others indiscriminately given by the Government, forgotten.[104]

And after describing the number of forms to be filled up, the grouping according to occupation, etc: 'All of this, of course, seemed to us extremely unfair'.

Demobilisation proper began on January 11, after inconceivable muddle in the regulations for the order of release had exasperated the men by their injustice, and reduced the officers to a state of despair in the attempt to understand them aright. February 2 brought the first rational order, giving precedence to men who had enlisted before January 1916, or were over 37 years old, or had been wounded three times or more.[105]

An unusual insight is also provided by a report given on 7 January to the Ashton and Stalybridge Trades Council by William Headock, who had toured the western battle zone, as a delegate of the Lancashire and Cheshire Cardroom Workers' Amalgamation, in a trade union delegation comprising representatives of various unions. He had

> found great unrest among the soldiers. Men who had served throughout the war contended that they should be the first to be demobilised. The delegates were repeatedly asked: 'When are they going to demobilise us?' Many said that if the Government did not demobilise them very soon, 'they would demobilise themselves'.[106]

There was an eloquent expression of how the upper ranks of the army viewed the soldiers' feelings in a memorandum on demobilisation drawn up by the Army's General Headquarters in France and submitted to the Secretary of State for War (Winston Churchill) by Sir Henry Wilson, on 14 January 1919:

> The Press has been allowed to run wild on the subject of demobilisation. Statements have been made which have no foundation in fact. Promises have been made in official pronouncements by the Ministry of Labour which are not in accordance with the orders issued by the Army Council. An influential part of the Press – notably the *Daily Mail, Daily Express* and other cheap papers, which circulate widely in the Army – have published articles abusing the military authorities and undermining discipline. Speed in demobilisation has been made an election cry. In consequence of all this incitement and uncertainty, there have been disturbances and passive resistance in England. These disturbances have, according to the Press, succeeded in their object of securing the release of the agitators, and have therefore already spread to the bases in France.[107]

There was, the paper stated, 'unrestfulness among all ranks due to the conviction that faith has been broken with them over (i) the Election (ii) demobilisation'.

In the private diaries kept by serving soldiers there is also some evidence before the end of 1918 of the 'unrestfulness' of which Sir Henry Wilson had written – not directly connected with a demand for demobilisation, but obviously bearing on it. Sergeant Buckeridge, whose diary for 11 November has already been quoted, (on page 4) added soon afterwards:

> There was a riot in our Division here [Warghams le Petit]. The fellows declined to march and carry full packs. The war was over for them, and they declined to be pack animals any longer. It all seemed very foolish to me, but the authorities very wisely conceded what was asked for, and in the end spare gear was carried for us.

The diarist also mentioned, without further details 'riots' at Bovay (? Beauvais?) over bad rations 'and delay in reaching homes'. At Cambrai, where his unit was in barracks before going on leave, he found that 'the feelings was no better . . . It seemed as though the whole Army had become imbued with a spirit of revolt against the system which had held the individual so firmly for so long'.

Captain A. E. Bundy, of 2nd Battalion, Middlesex Regiment, was impressed by precisely that feeling at Salonika, as his diary for the six weeks from 17 November to 24 December shows:

> Strangely enough, now that the war is over, numbers of the men refuse to obey orders, or rather they show a certain amount of independence that is most disconcerting. I had to talk to a whole company of men that were disgracefully abusive to their officers. I realised that any show of military authority would be fatal, so I reasoned with them and told them that for the benefit of all, and in order to facilitate the movement of those who were anxious to get back to England, it was necessary that they should still behave as disciplined soldiers. My remarks were greeted by catcalls and rude noises . . . So I announced that I should look to the men themselves for cooperation, and that if there was obstruction I should have the offenders arrested *and kept back*. There was then almost complete silence, and I had no further difficulty ['kept back' was certainly the most compelling argument].

This diary, like that of Sergeant Buckeridge, is in the Imperial War Museum.

FRANCE

Here, in the base nearest to Britain, the first of the 'disturbances' – and so far the most documented – took place.

At 11.30 a.m. on 28 January 1919, the general in command of the 5th Army was ordered to move an infantry brigade (less one battalion) of the 35th Division 'at once to *Calais* for special duty'. Less than two hours later, the entire brigade had to be sent. After 11 p.m. that night, the remainder of the 35th Division and also the 31st Division, both without their artillery, were also ordered 'for special duty' to the neighbourhood of Calais. In the meantime, three Guards machine-gun battalions from the 1st and 3rd Armies were transferred to the 5th Army, to be concentrated 'forthwith' in the neighbourhood of St Omer (itself not far from Calais). On the next day, 29 January, four battalions of the 3rd Army were sent for duty at the bases of Etaples, Le Havre, Rouen and Abbeville. In the next few days the troops already at Rouen and Etaples were reinforced, and others were sent to Cherbourg. However, by the beginning of the second week in February the flurry had subsided, and most of the troops sent to Calais were withdrawn.[108]

What had caused these sudden concentrations at the British army bases in France? The dreary language of the Adjutant-General's war diaries gives the official answer, which may be summarised as follows:[109]

On Monday, 27 January, the Army Ordnance Corps and the railwaymen at Calais struck because a private had been arrested 'for making a seditious speech'. He was temporarily released and next day was brought back to camp; whereupon the railwaymen resumed working. But now 5000 men who had been on leave in England and had been held up by the rail strike went on strike themselves. They demanded the right to return to England with ten days' leave to seek employment (as had happened in Great Britain). They repeated these demands to the base commandant and another general, who addressed them in the afternoon. Evidently these generals had promised to communicate with higher authorities: for at another mass meeting at 7.30 p.m. in the evening they told the soldiers that their demands could not be granted, but that 'an officer from General Headquarters would investigate demobilisation grievances'. The soldiers refused to accept this, and sent three delegates to accompany the general back to the base headquarters.

Late that evening they were informed that nothing more could be done, and they returned to their camps.

But that evening (28 January) three battalions arrived from the 105th Infantry Brigade, and, beginning with next morning, there arrived the 31st and 33rd Divisions in their entirety. 'The Officer commanding the Leave Camp was ejected by the men during the morning.' But at 2 p.m. General Byng, commander of the 3rd Army, arrived and took charge. After talking with the soldiers' representatives for two hours, he ordered a further conference for 11 a.m. next day (30 January). But at that hour the 35th Division 'reinstated the Commandant of the Base Camp, occupied the camp, and arrested four ringleaders. The remainder of the leave men proceeded to their units in the course of the day'.

From the correspondence of Sir Douglas Haig with Winston Churchill we learn that, while the two divisions mentioned earlier surrounded the camp with machine-guns ready, the 104th Brigade of the 35th Division marched into the camp with fixed bayonets, herded the 'mutineers' into one end of it, and arrested their leaders. Haig (according to his diary) wanted to shoot the arrested men, but was prevented by Churchill, who realised that bloodshed would create great trouble at home.[110] The men were court-martialled and sentenced to various terms of imprisonment.

In the meantime, the Ordnance Corps men's grievances were discussed by their delegates and the general already mentioned, together with various other officers, for five hours on 30 January. A number of the men's demands were evidently acceptable for transmission to the War Office – a thirty-six-hour week, improvement of rations and pay, and the speeding up of demobilisation. But the military authorities refused to recognise the Soldier's Council which had been formed, since it was 'unnecessary'. Women nurses of the QMRAC had also put forward demands, particularly that women police should be appointed. There is no indication of the reply to this demand, or to the men's request for permission to attend an Albert Hall meeting in London in February. (This was the all-in 'Hands Off Russia!' demonstration called by the British Socialist Party for 8 February, at which, among others, John Maclean, George Lansbury, Lady Warwick, the writer Israel Zangwill, Sylvia Pankhurst and Cathal O'Shannon of the Irish Transport and General Workers' Union spoke.)

Work was resumed on 31 January.

From the recollections of one man who played a significant part in these events, a number of additional details can be drawn:[111]

'The Calais mutiny had its origin in the Valdelièvre workshops: the men were mainly artisans and largely trade unionists enrolled in the RAOC.' About twelve months before the end of the war, after a negotiating committee had failed to secure an agreement that the working day should end at 5 p.m. instead of 6 p.m., a walkout at the earlier hour was called for. This failed, because the response was only partial, and the chief organiser – a staff sergeant – was transferred and probably victimised. However, the working day was shortened by half an hour. There were 2000 men in the camp.

'Nevertheless, discontent continued, and Government war propaganda lecturers have good reason to remember the towsing they received – one of the effects of reading Socialist publications which were smuggled into the camp.' During the General Election of December 1918 there was an attempt to prevent the weekly *Herald* from coming into the camp (newspapers there being distributed free to soldiers as potential voters). But this was frustrated by two soldiers who went into the town, commandeered the whole stock and distributed it in camp. 'The effect was electrical – it was like starving men reaching out for food.' A committee composed of one from each hut was formed immediately, to take orders and arrange distribution. Very soon afterwards 200 copies of each issue were going into the camp, to be read by three times that number of soldiers.

The events described in the official records quoted above were precipitated by the arrest at 4 p.m. on 2 January of one of the soldiers prominent in the agitation over demobilisation and his immediate sentencing for 'malingering'. At once a crowd of soldiers went to the C.O. to try and persuade him to release the prisoner, and when this failed broke open the guardroom and released the man themselves. An attempt to rearrest him at 10.30 p.m. was frustrated in the same way:

> Failing in this, imported military police then arrested the sergeant of the guard for failing to prevent the release of the prisoner. Our blood was up now with a vengeance, and the sergeant was soon released. A thoroughly frightened C.O. promised to meet the committee and go into all grievances. The next day, after the meeting with the committee, many concessions were made, including that of hours.

However, a few days later 'a hardening in the attitude of the officers was noticeable'. But this had been expected, and efforts were made to organise other camps in the area. On Sunday, 12 January, came the news that the same man had been arrested when leaving a Royal Engineers camp, and hurried to the town jail. A strike was immediately called for the next morning (Monday, 13 January):

> Although, as prearranged, every man was on the parade ground, not one fell in when the bugle sounded, and our pickets had already taken the place of the sentries. During the morning, news came that at Vendroux 2,000 men were all out, and were marching down that afternoon. They arrived headed by the regimental band and with all their NCO's participating. Both camps then joined in a march on the headquarters of the Calais area to interview Brigadier-General Rawlinson. Our bands were in attendance, and the frightened French shopkeepers put up their shutters as 4,000 very determined men marched through the streets. The headquarters were surrounded and a deputation entered.
>
> After a futile attempt to induce the besieging army to withdraw, the general agreed to release our comrade, who had been transferred elsewhere, and that he should be in the camp by Tuesday midday. The deputation resolutely refused to discuss any of our grievances or to call off the strike until our comrade had been released.

In fact, he was brought in by car at the time agreed, and 'was received with joyous acclamation'. In the meantime, parties of picked men had gone out to all other camps in the area, large and small, and found them all solid: about 20,000 men in all were out. There were strike committees functioning in all the camps, with a headquarters office at Valdelièvre issuing daily 'orders' and even permits.

When General Byng arrived – to deal with the 'malcontents' at the leave camps – he had infantry introduced into the workshops and machine-gun units posted in the RAOC camps. 'However, the tactics of fraternising with Byng's army were adopted, and with surprise we learned that they themselves had been in dispute just previously, mainly over the question of demobilisation.' Finally, the conference described in the official records was held, thirteen heads of different departments meeting thirteen men and women representing the soldiers' side. It lasted until 10 p.m. Most of the soldiers' demands were accepted, but others were to be forwarded to the War Office.[112] The delegation agreed to this – but when most of the men at Valdelièvre returned that night from a special cinema show they found to their consternation that a minority, left in camp, had 'voted' to end the strike. Other camps, on hearing of this, followed suit.

However, although work was resumed next day, neither the military police nor anyone else tried to suppress the committee, which was now called 'The Calais Area Soldiers' and Sailors' Association', with four or more delegates from the larger camps and two each from the smaller ones. It met in cafés, twenty to thirty servicemen regularly attending:

> However, the military authorities had had their lesson, and about three weeks after the strike demobilisation commenced in real earnest . . . Thus ended what we have reason to believe was the most complete and best organised revolt in the modern history of the British Army.

The author of this account added that the man whose arrest had led to the strike had been confined in a damp cell, handcuffed and in leg-irons. As a consequence, he contracted pneumonia and died in hospital. 'A sum of £150 was collected among the men for his widow and two children.' The man was Private John Pantley of Royal Army Ordnance Corps; he died on 13 February 1919, aged thirty-two.

It must be emphasised that this account in the weekly *Workers' Life*, corresponding in all essentials with what emerges from the official records, did not deal with the strike of the 5000 men on leave. Indeed, its writer said that he had been unable to discover where or when the court-martial of the four 'ringleaders' of the leave men had taken place. Nor had he been able to discover the facts about other 'rebellions' that took place at *Boulogne, Etaples* and elsewhere.

On *Etaples*, however, there are vivid memories in the diary of Mr Calcutt, who was quoted earlier (on page 4). His battalion was at this town on 9 January 1919. On returning to his unit from hospital, he found the following state of affairs:

Battalion doing nothing. They have had trouble with discipline. HQ Company sent in a round robin asking for an objectionable officer to be removed. All the NCO's reduced. C Company demonstrated. Put the wind up the CO., who postponed the 'criming session' for the Round Robiners, and went and saw the Brigadier instead. C Company tore down the Company flag and threw it in the ditch. The Brigadier told the C.O. he was lucky. He had got his officers *with* him. He said most Battalions had not! C.O. sent for 7 men per Company to state grievances. Demand for flag back unlucky as French children have got it. As a result, all the packs were carried on the trek all the way, and the Battalion only had rifle inspection.

There are also fleeting references to such events in the official records. Thus, a report on a visit to the embarcation camps at *Le Havre* (13 January 1919) says: 'I understand that on one occasion a party refused to entrain on account of demobilisation grievances.' The writer also speaks witheringly of 'the British policy of demobilisation, the tendency of which to kaleidoscopic change could not fail to embarrass the work'.[113] The war diary of the 5th Army's General Staff mentioned among the emergency measures taken on 28–30 January 1919, under orders from General Headquarters (30 January), that the 176th Infantry Brigade Headquarters, the 17th Royal Sussex, the 25th Liverpools, and the 26th Royal Welsh Fusiliers were moved by rail to *Dunkirk* for duty at the base.[114] This seems to echo a remark by B. G. A. Carvell (who was working as clerk at the Army Ordnance Corps Depot, Vendroux, at the time) in his recollections of January 1919, that the 178th Brigade at *Dunkirk* had prepared to go on strike, but immediate demobilisation was promised, and no action was taken.[115]

The papers of Colonel B. H. Puckle, mentioned earlier (the originals are preserved in the Oxfordshire County Archives), also contain a reference to the kind of dissatisfaction which was prevalent in the first week of January 1919 – although it must be said that the grievances which he described did not include the delay over demobilisation. As, however, his unit was stationed near Calais, that question cannot be completely excluded. Colonel Puckle had been recalled from leave unexpectedly by his second in command, and noted on 9 January:

I have seen two of my officers on their way home on leave, and I gather from what they have told me that the reason why I have been recalled is that the men have been misbehaving themselves and refusing to do this, that and the other thing. However I don't think it can be anything very serious, as they haven't sent a car to meet me.

Two days later, after reaching his unit, he wrote:

The reason I was recalled was that the battalion had become a bit fed up with the last billets, and had refused to do one or two things, such as company drill with equipment and so on. Nothing serious . . . It all could have been settled at once without any difficulty, and everything was peaceful by the time I arrived.

EN ROUTE FOR RUSSIA

There is a curious account of one frustrated expression of discontent over demobilisation, directly connected with intervention in Russia. Mr F. R. Banks, wrote of an incident while he was at sea, apparently in February 1919:

When the motor-mechanics heard of the impending operations in Russia, their C.P.O. ringleader, a former shop steward in Austins, demanded to see the S.B.N.O. to request their return home for demobilisation. When I asked this man how long he and others had been in the service he replied: 'Since January'. When I asked: 'Which January?' he replied: 'January 1918'. They were the conscripts of the war, and though some were good enough fellows there were the usual disgruntled ones and sea lawyers. I told them that they had only been in the service a dog-watch, but I would see the SBNO and put their request before him – giving me the chance of seeing him alone and warning him of the position. He played up well, saw the whole crowd, and told them that if they did not obey orders they would face a charge of mutiny. He was very impressive in going into what would happen if the charge were proved. So somewhat crest-fallen they returned to quarters.[116]

It will be noticed that neither the 'sea lawyers' nor the naval officers knew of, or at any rate referred to – the government's pledge, a full month before, that only volunteers would be sent to Russia!

ARCHANGEL

On 3 March 1919, Lieutenant-Colonel Radcliffe, Assistant Director of Military Operations, reported to the Deputy Chief of the Imperial General Staff on the 'unreliable state of the troops comprising the forces under the command of Generals Ironside and Maynard' (i.e. in the Archangel and Murmansk areas). They were 'a heterogeneous assortment of all nationalities . . . tired, dispirited, homesick and inclined to be mutinous', and their low morale made them accessible to the 'very active and insidious Bolshevik propaganda'.

This pessimistic report might have been interpreted as referring only to the French, American, White Russian and Polish soldiers under British command, but for Radcliffe's request that many 'specially selected officers of the highest stamp should be sent out as soon as possible' [more than likely referring to *British* officers] and that the generals be authorised to announce that 'all men entitled to demobilisation will be replaced at the earliest possible moment' – which most certainly could only refer to *British* troops.[117]

The 'very active and insidious Bolshevik propaganda' at this time was taking the form of a four-page English-language newspaper, which found its way weekly into all kinds of unexpected places behind the British and American lines. Its title was the *Call* – not entirely accidental, since its subtitle said that it was 'the organ of the English-speaking group of Communists in Russia'. Their outstanding and most experienced member was Joe Fineberg, a member of the executive committee of the British Socialist Party (formerly the Social-Democratic Federation) until he was deported to Russia in 1918, and the most practised writer and speaker in the English-speaking group. The organ of the BSP since Easter 1916 had been the *Call* – and Fineberg had obviously suggested that the title be borrowed.

The front page of the issue of 15 January (no. 18) carried as its banner headline: 'Allies Press Germany to Fight Russia'. It was based on German reports that the German Armistice Commission and the Allied military authority had been discussing this very proposition. But in fact the Armistice signed on 11 November, as noted earlier, contained two clauses providing that German troops should remain where they were in the territories of the former Russian Empire until the Allies were satisfied that 'order' had been restored, i.e. that the Bolsheviks had been crushed. And we now know, thanks to Mr Martin Gilbert, that on the day *before* the Armistice was signed, Winston Churchill considered that 'we might have to build up the German Army, as it was important to get Germany on her legs again for fear of the spread of Bolshevism'. On 10 January 1919 he had urged in Cabinet that they should 'let Germany know that, if she were prepared to organise her Eastern front against the ingress of Bolshevism, the Allied Governments would raise no objection'. And only a little later (9 April 1919) he wrote to Lloyd George that his policy would be: 'Free Germany; fight Bolshevism; make Germany fight Bolshevism'.[118]

So Bolshevik propaganda may have been 'insidious': but it was true.

On 22 January the *Call* (no. 19) had as its front-page headline: 'Soviet Government offers Peace to Allies'. It quoted Reuter and the Paris *Humanité* as the authority that such a peace offer had been made. It included the proposal for an armistice and for the opening of negotiations without barring any questions at issue . . . The Allied Governments had refused to consider the offer. The issue also quoted the editorials of the Liberal *Westminster Gazette* and the Tory *Weekly Dispatch*, which had opposed the continuation of intervention.

In fact, as was shown earlier, the *Daily Express* had been denouncing intervention, too.

Thus the Bolshevik propaganda may have been 'insidious': but it was founded on facts – and the facts had already, by the time the article appeared, led to widespread action by British troops at home.

On 29 January the front page of the *Call* (no. 20) was devoted to the murder in Berlin of Rosa Luxemburg and Karl Liebknecht, the German Communist leaders. But on its back page it printed the official protest of the Soviet Government against the Allies' decision that Russian prisoners of war in German hands should be handed over to them, instead of being free to return to their own country, and against the attempts being made in Hungary and the Balkans to force prisoners to enrol in the White forces. It printed the unanimous resolution of the French Socialist Party's leadership (which was anti-Bolshevik) demanding 'the recall of Allied troops from Russia'. And it exposed the fantastic stories about the 'nationalisation of women in Russia' which were then circulating in Britain, on the authority of Major-General Poole (at Archangel). This propaganda may have been 'insidious', but it provided British soldiers in North Russia with facts.

On 5 February the *Call* (no. 21) for the first time printed reports (received from abroad by radio or via the German and Dutch press, since all direct communications with Britain had been severed by the Allied occupation of Archangel the previous August) about the soldiers' strikes at Osterley, Brighton, Folkestone and Dover, as well as the demonstration at Whitehall. On 22 February (no. 22) it printed additional information of this movement, based on Reuter wireless news: the demonstrations at Fairlop and Shoreham were described, together with a selection of quotations from leading articles in the British and French papers opposing intervention, among them the *Daily News*, the *Manchester Guardian*, *Le Matin* and *Petit Journal*. Not less 'insidious', probably, was the two-column official reply of the Soviet Government on 4 February accepting an Allied invitation (made under popular pressure) to attend peace negotiations at Prinkipo Island in the Sea of Marmora. The Allies had sent it out by radio, without any direct intimation to the Soviet Government (and they dropped it immediately when the Whites refused to come).[119]

All this was propaganda by facts: it may have been 'insidious', even 'very active' – but it happened to be true. The *Call* was published from mid-September 1918 until the beginning of 1920.

Whether for this reason or for any other, at least one expression of 'mutinous' inclinations among the British troops was recorded in official papers (Colonel Radcliffe gave no instance himself). On 23 February 1919 General Ironside cabled to the War Office from Archangel:

> Yesterday the mobile company of the 13th Yorkshires reached Seletskoye [in the advanced position of the Allied forces, about 100 miles south of Archangel], and on being ordered to move up to Srednemechenga [a few miles further on] in relief and support of Russian and other British troops, they refused to go. The O.C. Battalion informs me the men are quite orderly . . . Lieut. Col. Lavie, who is newly appointed to the battalion, reported to me about a week ago on his arrival here that when the orders to move to Archangel command became known, the men of this company

refused to go, and that he talked to them for about an hour, after which his orders were carried out quietly . . . I can tell the men that they will only be required to carry out offensive operations if they are absolutely essential, and that the positions we now occupy must be held for the safety of the whole force. I have told them that the whole question of Russia is being considered, and that they must do their duty for the honour of the British Empire meanwhile.

However, next day the general cabled that the company still refused to move: the other companies had obeyed orders, he believed without question.

On 27 February he reported:

I have just got back from Seletskoye where for a short time I found a quite serious situation. A soldiers' meeting was held, which was joined only by some ASC and RAMC, besides one company of the 13th Battalion Yorkshires and a few men from another company: and although the men were orderly they were very obstinate and persistent. I have [group omitted] some 3[?] non-commissioned officers and 30 men for court-martial. This battalion has a new colonel who dealt with the situation well. He has just come from a senior officers' school, the trouble being long-standing, and before sailing for Russia a slight trouble occurred at Dundee.

On 3 March he added:

The ill-discipline of the 13th Battalion Yorkshires is now settled, and when I saw them off from Seletskoye to Srednemechenga they were quite cheery. The ringleaders consisting of 3 NCO's, one a regular, and about 5 men are being dealt with. No further trouble with this battalion is anticipated.

Whether on account of this event, or because of the general feeling among the troops, the War Office cabled to General Ironside four days later that the War Cabinet had decided to recommend the evacuation of Archangel at the earliest possible moment to the Allied Governments.[120]

In his book on the Archangel invasion Field-Marshal Lord Ironside described the affair pretty fully. He added that Colonel

Lavie had been told by two sergeants, at a parade of the battalion unarmed, that 'the battalion would do no more fighting', whereupon he ordered a lance-corporal to take a file of men to fetch their rifles. When they did so, he put the sergeants under close arrest and sent them to the guardroom. Interviewing the two sergeants, Ironside told them they would be brought before a court-martial. He added in his book that they had served in the Royal Army Pay Corps in England all through the war until March 1918, when they were transferred to the Yorkshires and thus to Murmansk. At the court-martial they were sentenced to be shot, but: 'In accordance with my secret orders from His Majesty that no death sentences were to be carried out after the Armistice, I commuted their sentence to life imprisonment, and they were taken down to the base to start serving these sentences'.[121]

The author did not mention the other NCO and the five privates on whom he had reported to the War Office – nor anything further about the two men who had been sentenced. It is noteworthy, however, that he went on immediately to say that both officers and men of this unit were serving 'in a political struggle of which they understood nothing' – and, although he made light of such outbreaks as not important in themselves (there was one a few days later in a French battalion on leave at Archangel), he admitted that

> we are drawing terribly near to the end of our tether as an efficient fighting force ... both officers and men were anxious about their future prospects in civil life. Every letter they received from home made them feel that they were missing the labour market. Boredom amongst those who were not fighting, combined with the numbing effect of the cold and darkness, had brought them to a state of exasperation with which it was very difficult to deal.[122]

A little more light on the affair of the 13th Yorkshires was cast by an entry in Bruce Lockhart's diary on 3 September 1931: 'Had a long talk with Thornhill about Russia. He also told me that at Archangel the 13th battalion of the Yorkshire Light Infantry revolted and set up a Soviet. Two sergeants were given fifteen years. They should be coming out now.'[123]

It will be seen that the state of mind of the soldiers at Archangel recorded by Lord Ironside corresponded by and large with that which was manifested by the soldiers in Britain. And if its expressions were more limited at the invasion front than they had been, some five weeks before, at home, this must have been due to the possibility that strict military discipline would be enforced in the way described by the Field-Marshal. The key words in his narrative, however, are 'a political struggle of which they understood nothing'.

INDIA

Among the papers preserved in Mr Peter H. Liddle's *1914–1918 Archive* are those of Sergeant J. Davey, Royal Engineers. An old Regular soldier, he had joined the army in March 1906, and had seen service in France for nearly a year in 1914–15 and then in Mesopotamia for thirty months. With his unit he had left Basra for Karachi in March 1919, expecting to go to England. But at Karachi, in April, the troops were addressed by the General Officer Commanding the district. Mr Davey describes the scenes:

> The riots had broken out in the Punjaub, in places such as Amritzar, Jullander, Ludianha: and he trusted each of us would be ready to move north to be a protection for the white women and children in those parts . . . With the war against the Central Powers of Europe over, and the Armistice in being some months with those various countries, the GOC's remarks were taken up at once on the parade, by one soldier requesting permission to be able to pose a question on the spot. This being granted, he quite politely said: 'As the white persons up country were there presumably from choice, and the war for which the men had joined up was over, didn't he, the General, think it time the troops held up in India were sent home, finished with war, so that they might see how their wives and families were faring, after a matter of their men folk being away in many cases up to 4 years?!'
> The question, being a fair and politely put one, was accepted in good part, but it did not stop us being organised into 'special' Infantry Battalions.

There was no question of a strike here, of course, but a faithful report of this unusual public debate might easily have strengthened the Prime Minister's decision to hurry on with demobilisation.

NOTES

1 *Daily Express*, 6 January 1919.
2 *Daily Chronicle*, 6 January 1919.
3 *Daily News*, 6 January 1919.
4 *The Times*, 6 January 1919.
5 *Evening News*, 3 January 1919.
6 *Daily Mail*, 6 January 1919.
7 *The Times*, loc. cit.
8 Ibid.
9 *Morning Post*, 6 January 1919.
10 *Herald*, 11 January 1919.
11 *The Times*, loc. cit.
12 *Morning Post*, loc. cit.
13 *Belfast Telegraph*, 6 January 1919.
14 *The Times*, 6 January 1919.
15 *Daily Chronicle*, 6 January 1919.
16 *The Times*, 6 January 1919.
17 *Daily Telegraph*, 7 and 8 January 1919.
18 *The Times*, 7 January 1919.
19 *Morning Post*, 7 January 1919.
20 *Daily Telegraph*, 8 January 1919.
21 *Daily Telegraph*, 9 January 1919.
22 *The Times*, 8 January 1919.
23 *Daily Telegraph*, 9 January 1919.
24 *Kent Messenger*, 11 January 1919.
25 *Daily News*, 11 January 1919. The same account, in all essentials, was given by Graham Wallace, *RAF Biggin Hill* (London: 1957).
26 *Daily News*, 10 January 1919.
27 *Westminster Gazette*, 11 January 1919.
28 *Daily Chronicle*, 9 January 1919.
29 *Daily Telegraph*, 7 January 1919.
30 *Manchester Guardian*, 7 January 1919.
31 *The Times*, 7 January 1919.
32 *Manchester Guardian*, loc. cit.
33 *The Times*, loc. cit.
34 *Daily News*, 7 January 1919.
35 *Pall Mall Gazette*, 6 January 1919.
36 *The Times*, 8 January 1919.
37 *Daily News*, 7 January 1919.
38 *Manchester Guardian*, loc. cit.
39 *Buckinghamshire Advertiser*, 10 January 1919.
40 *Evening Standard*, 7 January 1919.
41 Ibid.; *The Times*, 8 January 1919.
42 *Daily Telegraph*, 8 January 1919.
43 *Glasgow Herald*, 7 January 1919.
44 *Daily Mail*, 8 January 1919.
45 *Daily Telegraph*, 9 January 1919.
46 *Pall Mall Gazette*, 8 January 1919.

47 *Star*, 8 January 1919.
48 *The Times*, 8 and 9 January 1919; *Daily Telegraph*, 8 January 1919; *Daily Chronicle*, 8 January 1919.
49 *Daily Telegraph*, 7 January 1919.
50 *Daily Mail*, 7 January 1919.
51 *Sussex Daily News*, 7 January 1919.
52 *The Times*, 7 January 1919.
53 *Sussex Daily News*, 7, 8, 9 and 10 January 1919.
54 *Globe* (London), 7 January 1919.
55 *Daily Mail*, 8 January 1919.
56 *Aldershot News*, 10 January 1919.
57 *Daily Telegraph*, 8 January 1919.
58 *Daily Telegraph*, 9 January 1919.
59 *Hampshire Observer*, 11 January 1919.
60 *Daily News*, 8 January 1919.
61 *The Times*, 17 January 1919.
62 *Isle of Wight County Press* (Newport) 11 January 1919.
63 *Shanklin Gazette*, 10 January 1919. It seems probable that the statement in Tom Bell's *British Communist Party* (London: 1937) p. 39, about a clash between 4000 soldiers and the police, in which several were killed and wounded, 'at Ryde, in the Isle of Wight', is based on a misunderstanding. Such an event could not have been left out of the press or memoirs of the time – and Bell quotes no source for the statement. But on 4 and 5 March 1919, several weeks after the British soldiers' strikes, there was such an event at Rhyl, in North Wales. At Kinmel Park Camp 19,000 Canadian soldiers were gathered, mostly after service in France; and several thousands of them did revolt against continued delays in their promised demobilisation. After a mass meeting, they destroyed practically all the shops and shot dead or wounded several officers and police. Order was restored only after the War Office promised that half would be sent home in a few days, and the rest shortly afterwards. No British soldiers were involved (*The Times*, 7 and 8 March 1919, and subsequent days).
64 Andrew Boyle, *Trenchard* (London: 1962) pp. 312–28.
65 *Pall Mall Gazette*, 7 January 1919; *The Times*, 8 January 1919.
66 *The Times*, 13 January 1919; *Western Daily Press* (Bristol) 13 January 1919.
67 *Daily Telegraph*, 13 January 1919.
68 *Western Morning News* (Plymouth) 9 January 1919.
69 *Daily Telegraph*, 7 January 1919.
70 *The Times*, 11 January 1919.
71 *Western Morning News*, 11 January 1919.
72 *Cornish Echo* (Falmouth) 10 January 1919.
73 *South Wales News* (Cardiff), 7 January 1919.
74 *Cambria Daily Leader* (Swansea) 9 January 1919.
75 *Salisbury Times and South Wiltshire Gazette*, 10 January 1919.
76 *WO 162. 14. p. 220.*
77 *Sunday Mercury* (Birmingham), 5 January 1919.
78 *Daily Telegraph*, 9 January 1919.
79 *Manchester Guardian*, 9 January 1919.
80 *Star*, 7 January 1919; *Bedford Daily Circular*, 8 January 1919.

81 *Bedfordshire Times and Independent*, 10 January 1919.
82 Ibid., 14 and 31 January 1919.
83 *Wellingborough News*, 17 January 1919.
84 *Grantham Journal*, 18 January 1919.
85 *Yorkshire Post*, 11 January 1919.
86 *PRO WO 95, Box 5459.*
87 *Manchester Guardian*, 10 January 1919; *Yorkshire Post*, 10 January 1919.
88 *Daily News*, 10 January 1919; *Manchester Guardian*, 10 January 1919.
89 *Manchester Guardian*, 11 January 1919.
90 *Daily News*, 14 January 1919; *Daily Telegraph*, 14 January 1919.
91 *Globe*, 9 January 1919; *Morning Post*, 10 January 1919.
92 *Newcastle Daily Chronicle*, January 11.
93 *Scotsman*, 9 January 1919; *Daily Telegraph*, 9 January 1919.
94 *Glasgow Herald*, 11 January 1919.
95 *Glasgow Citizen*, 11 January 1919.
96 *Scotsman*, 15 January 1919.
97 *Pall Mall Gazette*, 8 January 1919.
98 *Dundee Courier*, 8 January 1919.
99 *Morning Post*, 9 January 1919.
100 *Scotsman*, 9 January 1919.
101 *Morning Post*, 10 January 1919.
102 *History of the 50th Infantry Brigade* (London: 1919) pp. 118,˙121.
103 C. H. Ommaney, *War History of the 1st Northumbrian Brigade, R.F.A.(T.F.)* (Newcastle-upon-Tyne: 1927) pp. 244–5.
104 S. L. Levy, *Memories of the 71st and 83rd Companies, R.A.S.C. (M.T.)* (London: 1931) p. 131.
105 O'Hanlon, *Plain History of the 6th (Service) Battalion, Dorsetshire Regiment* (London: 1931) p. 187.
106 *Manchester Guardian*, 8 January 1919.
107 *PRO, WO 32, 5242* (memoranda on demobilisation).
108 Summarised from the General Staff reports at the Public Record Office, *WO 95. 23.*
109 *WO 95. 26.*
110 These particulars are given by M. Gilbert, *Winston S. Churchill*, IV (London: 1975) pp. 192–3.
111 'The Calais Mutiny', in *Workers' Life* (London) 29 March and 5 April 1929.
112 Carver, *A History of the 10th (Service) Battalion, East Yorkshire Regiment, 'Hull Commercials'*(Hull, 1937) – which was among those moved to Calais – wrote (p. 185), that the officers who met the soldiers' representatives on 30 January were headed by General Sir W. R. Birdwood, GCMG, GOC 5th Army.
113 WO 95. 41. GHQ. Quarter-Master General's War Diary.
114 WO 95.522.
115 *From Monk to Busman* (London: 1935) quoted by T. H. Wintringham, *Mutiny* (London: 1936) p. 83.
116 F. R. Banks, *I Kept No Diary* (Shrewsbury, 1978) p. 38.
117 *WO 33. 950. Diary of Events in Russia and Siberia*, p. 26.
118 Gilbert, op. cit., pp. 226, 233, 277.
119 A discussion among the Allied leaders (the Council of Ten) on 15 February 1919, once the Whites had refused to go to Prinkipo, produced enlightening

comments. It was an awkward situation, from which the (Allied) Council should get out of its troubles as discreetly and simply as possible. No further reference should be made to Prinkipo (Clémenceau). The question was how to 'finesse the situation against the Bolsheviks' (Colonel House, President Wilson's adviser). They should take steps to 'put the Bolsheviks in the wrong' (Foreign Secretary Balfour). All this is in *Foreign Relations of the United States* IV, (Washington: 1943) pp. 17–21.

120 WO 33. 966, European War, Secret Telegrams, Series H, vol. II, pp. 47–65. The official history of this regiment does not mention this affair in its war record of the 13th Battalion, which sailed from Dundee on 16 October 1918 and reached Murmansk on 28 November (H. C. Wylly, *The Green Howards in the Great War*, Richmond, Yorkshire, 1926). Interestingly enough, the commanding officer of the White forces at Archangel, General Marcushevsky, (of whom Field-Marshal Ironside speaks highly in his book) reported in his memoirs that, after the meeting of the 13th Yorkshires, the British authorities had arranged to turn the machine-guns of the White Russians against the British battalion 'in the event of an open mutiny': V. V. Marcushevsky, *The Karelo-Murmansk Territory*, no. 2, (Petrozavodsk: 1929) p. 2; quoted in *The Internationalists*, A. Y. Manusevich, ed. (Moscow: 1967) p. 558.

121 *Archangel, 1918–1919* (London: 1953) pp. 112–13.
122 Ibid., pp. 113–14.
123 Kenneth Young (ed.), *The Diaries of Sir Robert Bruce Lockhart*, I (London: 1973) p. 183.

4 'They Understood Nothing'

WHAT THE NEWSPAPERS THOUGHT

Almost everywhere, therefore, the first demand of the armed forces after the Armistice, where it found expression, was for demobilisation, now that the war in which they had enlisted or for which they had been conscripted was over. Even in those rare cases where there was no record of the general demand for an end to wartime petty restrictions or privations being accompanied by the call for demobilisation, there can be no reasonable doubt that in fact return to civil life was uppermost in the thought of most soldiers (and sailors) in January 1919. But so long as they were in uniform, there was also the possibility of being sent to the new theatre of war already in being in Russia: and it would be quite wrong to imagine that this prospect, too, because it was not everywhere publicly reported, was not present in the minds of those who organised or participated in the soldiers' strikes. For anyone who was in the forces at that time, and had the opportunity of hearing the conversations in huts and barracks, canteens and trains, there could be no possible doubt about the men's all-pervading worry.

True, in only a minority of the newspaper reports surveyed in earlier pages, did it figure publicly at Folkestone and Osterley, Aldershot, Park Royal and Bedford. But the comments in the provincial and local press *after* the weekend of 4–5 January made no secret of it, and this was all the more noticeable because among them were many newspapers which had previously said nothing about it. The following are some typical examples:

On 6 January the London *Pall Mall Gazette*, which had been carrying out a violent campaign for intervention until then, admitted that the feeling among the Army Service Corps men 'is attributed in many quarters to the oft-repeated rumour that plans are being prepared for sending a considerable force to Russia'. One of its reporters had been told by the soldiers at Downing Street that they had acted 'in a belief of a rumour that they were going to be dispatched forthwith to Russia'. Forgetful of its own report, barely three weeks earlier, that 'a thorough and conclusive spring campaign in Russia [is] apparently inevitable', the paper now called the rumour 'a ridiculous story'.

On 7 January the *Birmingham Gazette* wrote that

> some of the jingo papers . . . have called for a great expedition to Russia against the Bolsheviks, and it would be valuable to know how far the Army 'strikes' are an expression of dissatisfaction with the idea of the mysterious operations in Russia.

Among the letters it printed denouncing these operations was one from a reader, Fred Hobday, who said that he had had 'a number of letters from relatives of men who have been sent to Russia' after his previous letter attacking intervention had been printed on 31 December. The *Cambridge Daily News* editorial said:

> The moral of all the unrest, as far as the soldiers are concerned, is that they do not want to be kept indefinitely in the Army; and it is not at all surprising if, since Mr Thomas' disclosure of the feelings entertained in high quarters, they believe that the military authorities entertain designs that are not publicly expressed.

The Cardiff *Western Mail*, which was still in a cartoon demanding a 'Rescuer' to rescue captive 'Andromeda' – Russia – from a ferocious serpent 'Bolshevism', nevertheless for the first time tried to appease critics by saying that it was not suggesting the despatch of 'great armies', and that 'in due course' the Government hoped to replace the conscripts then in Russia by volunteers. The Plymouth *Western Morning News*, which as late as 4 January had been announcing that 'hordes of savages are descending upon civilisation: the scourge of the Huns was not worse', now confessed in its leading article that the soldiers 'show a strong repugnance to the thought of plunging into another war, this time against Russian Bolshevists'.

On 8 January the Dublin *Freeman's Journal* wrote: 'The unrest in the Army over the slowness of demobilisation and the prospect of a war in Russia is a grave symptom'. The *Birmingham Post* echoed its competitor of the day before:

> There is unrest arising from fear lest the Russian expedition should detain men in the Army who regard their obligations as at

end. The announcement now officially made [that no new drafts were being sent, only volunteers] should put an end to groundless apprehension on this score; but mischief has already been done by the uncertainty which must assuredly be reckoned among the causes of recent military discontent.

The *Bolton Evening News*, in its London letter, admitted: 'The flames of discontent among the troops waiting to be demobilised have undoubtedly been fanned by suggestions that they might be shipped off to Russia, there to begin a new war. The Government have hesitated to deny this statement.' Cardiff's *South Wales News*, which on 7 January had said that 'Britain cannot allow the Russian people to remain in a state of anarchy', now changed its tune, writing that 'not a little disquiet has arisen from an idea that numbers of our men were to be sent to Russia as an expeditionary force'. The Darlington *Northern Echo* wrote: 'It would be interesting to learn the exact value of the "military enterprise" in which 15,000 to 20,000 British troops are employed.' In most states, 'including Ireland', wrote the editorial, 'persons engaged in military enterprises not justified by a state of war are liable to very summary treatment if arrested' (thereby providing the soldiers with the argument that intervention was against the laws of war).

On 9 January the *Manchester Guardian* also gave direct encouragement to the soldiers. Its leading article said: 'Some units yesterday demanded the assurance that they would not be sent to Russia. Of course the soldier cannot be allowed to choose his destination, but fundamentally this demand is based on reason.'

On 10 January the *Sussex Daily News* (Brighton) printed its London correspondent's report: 'Any suggestion of increasing the strength of our armed forces in Russia would have excited restlessness in the Army.' The Bristol *Western Daily Press*, in its issue of 4 January, had written that 'the problem of the hour' seemed to be whether the Allies 'should require their soldiers, most of whom volunteered for one war, to serve in another of a very different character': and its 'London Letter' added that this would 'have to be on a much larger scale than some critics anticipate'. Now it printed the statement in its 'London Letter' that

> one of the causes of recent discontent was the feeling which had grown up that men in the Army, recruited for the period of the war, were still under an obligation to proceed to Russia or to other distant theatre of war if called upon.

At the same time 'it may now be definitely stated that from now onwards no more combatant troops of the present Army will be used for any purpose outside the Western theatre of operations'.

Not all these quite influential newspapers, spread far and wide over England and Wales, were in the habit of using biting and uninhibited language when writing of members of the Government, as was the custom of the Glasgow *Herald*. In its editorial comment on the appointment – announced on 11 January – of Winston Churchill as War Minister, the paper summed up very clearly both his identification, in the eyes of the soldiers, with the policy of war on Soviet Russia and the general feeling that his appointment meant the continuation of the war, whatever the soothing assurances inspired from Downing Street. The appointment, wrote the paper on 11 January,

> may be a blessing in disguise; but, if so, it will be the hardened opinion of a very large section of the public, and probably of at least 99 out of every 100 Army men with any knowledge of affairs, that never was disguise more effectual and complete.

It went on to refer to Churchill's personal military experience, but added that this 'would be heavily discounted by Mr Churchill's overweening self-assurance and his conspicuous gift of inspiring hostility and distrust by his instability and addiction to dubious adventure'. At the present time there were problems which required 'virtues possibly latent in him, but if so very successfully concealed'. One such problem in particular, said the paper, was that of demobilisation – in connection with which matters would not be materially improved 'by the new War Minister arraying himself in uniform and dashing off, say, to Archangel, to see if the campaign against the Bolshevists is being properly conducted'.

The most obvious conclusion, from this survey of newspaper comment *after* the strike movement among the soldiers had shown how universal was the feeling among '99 out of every 100 Army men', is that the strikes had had an extremely sobering effect on the politicians and their friends, the owners of newspapers. And, still more important, they had made a big and chastening impact upon the War Cabinet and the military chiefs.

The Socialist press, too, irrespective of its different trends, did not fail to bring out both the main striving of the soldiers – to get back to civilian life – and its particular importance for the fate of the armed attack on Soviet Russia (even if in many cases the soldiers did not dwell on it). George Lansbury's left-wing Labour weekly, *The Herald* – the wartime successor of his prewar unofficial Labour newspaper, the *Daily Herald* – wrote on 11 January 1919, in its political commentary, 'The Way of the World': 'The Army is in revolt against the red tabs and the red tapes. The war is over: they want to go home. That is the gist of the whole business.' Its editorial, however, went further:

> Have you wondered why demobilisation is so slow? Perhaps you think it is merely 'red tape'. It is not. It is the Red Flag – in Russia. Our rulers will not let the Army go because they are coquetting with the idea of using it against Russia 'on the grand scale'.

On 11 January, the weekly *Call* of the British Socialist Party – successor of the old SDF, as noted earlier in these pages, but, unlike the SDF, affiliated to the Labour Party – carried the front-page headline 'The Soldiers' Strike'. The article on that page, after summarising the news of the movement in the army, said:

> It is natural that the soldiers proclaim their discontent by agitation on matters vitally affecting them as soldiers. The very fact, however, that it is necessary for the press to deny the impending despatch of the soldiers to Russia shows that the demands of the Army are not confined to questions of demobilisation only.

Again, the paper's 'Notes and Comments' on political affairs remarked: 'The hostility of the soldiers to being used as an instrument for imposing an alien and predatory capitalism on the free Russian workers and peasants is not the least of the grievances now finding expression in the soldiers' ranks.'

The Independent Labour Party, with a number of MPs of its own elected as Labour Party candidates, carried more weight in the official machinery of the Labour movement. At first, in its issue of 9 January 1919, its weekly, the *Labour Leader*, confined itself to indicating the real purpose of sending the troops to Russia:

The Bolsheviks are fighting the Allies because the Allies, without any declaration of war, have invaded their land and mean to restore 'law and order', which means to restore the landlord and the financier to such a position that they can make profits out of Russia. For this the boys are stopped from coming back.

The following week, however, Philip Snowden, one of the ILP's most influential leaders and editor of its paper, was able to be more precise in his front-page 'Review of the Week'. The reports from several places enabled him to write: 'Some part of the soldiers' discontent was due to the impression that many of them were likely to be sent to Russia.'

IN THE WAR CABINET

Although, as was shown earlier, there were already differences within the War Cabinet on the question of how far intervention in Russia could go, it had made very little material difference to the policy before the soldiers themselves took action. In fact, nothing essential had changed since Sir Henry Wilson, as CIGS, had signed his paper on 5 December (setting out military commitments *'after peace is signed'* – i.e. for a long time ahead) to which reference has been made earlier.

But the events of 3 January and the following days caused the utmost alarm in the government, especially among the military authorities.

When, on Wednesday, 8 January, the demonstration of the 1500 Park Royal men in Downing Street took place, Sir William Robertson (commanding the Home Forces) reported that the men 'had put forward their grievances in reasonable language', and that some of their grievances might be genuine. The Prime Minister said he was quite willing to see their delegates, or the soldiers in a body. But Lord Milner (then still Secretary for War) thought this would be 'a bad precedent', encouraging similar 'processions' from other parts. The soldiers should be told that there were 'proper channels' for legitimate grievances; if this 'tendency to indiscipline and disorder' spread unchecked, the results might be serious. 'Disastrous', Sir Henry Wilson corrected him: this soldiers' delegation 'bore a dangerous resemblance to a Soviet'. The Prime Minister should not confer with it after the soldiers had disregarded their officers. General Feilding said that they had refused to accept his explanations, and he suggested that Sir William Robertson should see them and promise them that the PM would issue a statement on demobilisation. Near London there were about 50,000 ASC men, mostly 'not with much experience of strict Army discipline' (soon they would be demanding wages at civilian rates, Lord Weir anticipated). At present only a small minority were disaffected, Feilding said, but 'the agitation would spread if demonstrations were not prohibited'.

Lloyd George said they must be sure that any steps to this end were certain to be successful. Inevitably the position was one of great difficulty: 'between four and five millions of men had been undergoing for years the severe strain of war, with death confronting them. That strain had suddenly ceased, and a violent reaction was natural'. Sir Eric Geddes took up this line of thought. In order to keep a balance between rates of demobilisation at home and abroad, 'it had been necessary to keep men back at home who could be demobilised. *The men knew this, and feared that they were being kept back with a view to sending them to Russia*' [my italics].

Finally the War Cabinet decided (1) that Sir William Robertson should meet the delegates, (2) that officers should investigate the alleged grievances at Park Royal, and (3) that Lloyd George and Milner should prepare a press statement on demobilisation.[1]

This account of the War Cabinet meeting gives some idea of the impact which the soldiers' action had made by 8 January – the sixth day of the strikes. But other documents show that its full force had already been felt by at least one of the participants. On Monday, 6 January, Sir Henry Wilson had noted in his diary that he had got the other army leaders to support him in insisting that Lloyd George should make clear that the war was not over, and the soldiers must obey orders: 'otherwise we would have no army in a short time . . . if he doesn't do this the whole Army will be turned into a rabble'. Next day, he recorded, he told Lloyd George that he must back the War Office and the officers, and 'must crush out the poisonous part of the press'. And in making his way to the War Cabinet meeting on 8 January itself, he 'had to work my way through the soldiers to the door' (of No. 10 Downing Street) – a circumstance which evidently brought home to him more vividly what was going on.[2]

As the movement developed, Winston Churchill became more and more agitated, precisely because he realised – as of course did other Ministers – the adverse effect which granting the soldiers' demands would have upon the campaign in Soviet Russia. Wilson recorded on 10 January – Churchill's first day as Secretary for War – that he feared that the unrest would spread to other camps throughout the country, and that this would encourage Bolshevism in Britain.[3] At the War Cabinet that day, the Ministers had before them papers prepared by the War Office on North Russia and Siberia. Earlier (on 31 December), as already noted, the Imperial War Cabinet had decided, while not demobilising troops in Russia, not to reinforce them until the Allied Supreme War Council had discussed the whole situation. But now General Maynard was demanding more soldiers for this Murmansk campaign. The minute runs:

> General Wilson said that since that paper was written there had been signs of unrest in the Army at home, and it was notorious that the prospect of being sent to Russia was immensely unpopular. The result was that it was impossible for us to reinforce our troops in both Russia and Siberia.

He also complained that the situation had been aggravated by the lifting of censorship – to which Churchill responded by urging that it be 'resuscitated' at once. This was agreed to, which may explain a certain thinning-down of information in the press in the next few days.[4]

However, the debate at the meeting continued with a statement by Lord Curzon about the urgency of measures 'to stop the advance of Bolshevism before it penetrated Austria and Germany' mainly by sending money and munitions, as 'he believed it was most unlikely that volunteers would be forthcoming'. This at once brought Churchill in again. He hoped Curzon was wrong in his surmise about volunteers:

> A statement had appeared in the British Press to the effect that no British troops were to be sent to Russia. He thought this was unfortunate, and that a corrected statement should be made to the effect that no British troops would be sent to Russia unless they volunteered for that service.

It was on this occasion that he went on to make the suggestions, already mentioned, that defeated Germany might yet be drawn into war against Soviet Russia (an idea to which he was to turn again, twenty-five years later, in a very different situation).

At the same Cabinet, the question had arisen of the possible withdrawal of two battalions from Omsk. At once Churchill raised the alarm: 'The fabric we had been trying to construct would fall to pieces. The Czechs would go, Kolchak's army would disappear and the French would withdraw.' On this point, as on the earlier one, the matter was left to be discussed in Paris.

The argument went on from meeting to meeting, with the generals and Churchill doing their best to feed the flames – but with a growing opposition led by the Prime Minister. On 14 January Wilson was told by Haig and other generals that 'the state of the army is deplorable'.[5] Next day, at a War Office conference, Haig said that in the existing conditions the army was 'rapidly disappearing'.[6] On 14 January Churchill had cabled Ironside and Maynard that it was essential for their troops to stay in Russia, for their 'moral effect'; otherwise the whole fabric of Russo-Siberian 'resistance' would crumble. Now on 15 January, Churchill said the same thing to fifty journalists assembled at the War Office.[7] On 16 January he wrote to Austen Chamberlain, Chancellor of the Exchequer, that 'under the present pressure the Army is liquefying fast'. The next day, Sir Henry Wilson noted in his diary, the Chief of the Imperial General Staff told Churchill: 'We are sitting on the top of a mine which may go up at any minute.' Churchill himself wrote on 18 January to Lloyd George in Paris that Haig had told him of reports about discontent of the army in France (as has been seen, these reports were to prove justified ten days later). The following day Churchill cabled to Lloyd George in Paris that, if there were any further delay in settling the question of demobilisation, there would be nothing left of the army but a 'demoralised and angry mob'.[8] By 22 January Wilson was saying, 'We dare not give an unpopular order to the troops, and discipline is a thing of the past'; while Haig said, at a meeting of Ministers during the Premier's absence in Paris, that if the existing state of things continued, by the end of February he would have no army left in France.[9]

But by now Lloyd George was beginning to speak sharply to Churchill. On 17 January the latter's War Office advisers had produced a scheme under which, *apart* from the postwar Regular Army yet to be formed, all men enlisted in 1914 and 1915 were to be demobilised (a total of 2,700,000), but something like 1,200,000 of the rest were to be compulsorily retained, with better pay and conditions (250,000 at home, 650,000 in Western Europe and 250,000 in 'other theatres and garrisons').[10] Lloyd George cabled him, when he heard of this on 18 January, that the scheme might 'involve grave political consequences (it might even produce trouble in the Army)'. And in a telephone call on 21 January he repeated the latter warning, saying that the figures were 'extravagant'.[11] After the meeting of Ministers on 22 January, Lloyd George agreed to the figure of 1,200,000 men to be kept in the army, but with only ten divisions in France instead of fifteen, as had been suggested. Wilson entered in his diary next day that not a moment should be lost in making it clear that 1 million men would be retained, as all power over the army was slipping away. 'Of course if these men really refuse to serve, we are done: but I have no fear of this.'[12]

On 27 January Churchill wrote to Lloyd George, saying that Britain should continue the intervention, and reinforce its armies in Russia until victory was obtained: 'but unfortunately we have not the power – our orders would not be obeyed, I regret to say'.[13] Nevertheless, at the War Cabinet meeting on 28 January, Churchill pressed once more for more British troops to be sent to north Russia and Siberia. At that time there were 14,000 there in all – a 'most unsatisfactory' situation: it was not enough to enable the British troops 'to hold their own with confidence against the Bolshevik armies, which were growing in efficiency and audacity'. He demanded a free hand to take a bold and open line: and was supported by Geddes, who declared that it was essential

> to kill the hopes of the men who were expecting to get out of the Army at once . . . So long as the men at the front relied on the hope of getting back shortly to England, they would move heaven and earth to obtain their discharge.

Churchill, however, failed to get his free hand.[14] In a letter to Churchill, Bonar Law, his deputy, had admitted the previous day that he was 'terrified', and Wilson told Lloyd George he favoured 'getting ready to clear out of Murmansk and Archangel next summer'.[15]

It is obvious that the strikes and demonstrations in the army had served as a chastening cold shower to the advocates of what *The Times* less than four weeks earlier had called 'coming into conflict with Bolshevism in Russia', and enforcing the decree of the Peace

Conference (not yet assembled) 'by military means if necessary'. On 3 February, Churchill was still pressing Lloyd George to send more men to north Russia, but the Premier agreed only that auxiliaries 'to secure the health, comfort and nourishment of the troops there' should go. Lloyd George reminded Churchill that the War Cabinet had decided not to send reinforcements to Russia because their military advisers had said that 'there was considerable unrest in the Army on the subject of Russia, and that the dispatch of further troops might have serious results'.[16]

Wilson noted in his diary on 7 February that 'a certain amount of trouble' was still arising from time to time in connection with soldiers on leave who were due to return to the Continent, and the Army Council had consequently decided on bringing home the Guards division, an extreme measure.[17]

What was the 'certain amount of trouble'? On this there is a picturesque report in the reminiscences at the Imperial War Museum of Mr A. W. Fenn, of the 2nd Battalion, the Suffolk Regiment – an old Regular soldier from April 1910, who had been in the retreat from Mons during the first period of the war. He wrote:

> In late January 1919 I went on what was to be my last leave, and very hectic it proved to be. On 7 February I arrived at Victoria Station and was told no boats were running for a few days, and was told to go home for another week. But there were thousands of Scottish soldiers and Colonial troops, Canadian, Australian, etc. who were too far from home and were stranded in London with no money. They mutinied and tried to set fire to the Railway Transport Officers' office and wreck the station. They sent for Lt. Gen. Feilding commanding the London district. He tried to reason with them but they would have none of it. In fact they abused him and called him a bloody Brass Hat. They said take it off you are talking to fighting soldiers now. They fixed bayonets and held up all the traffic and said we will go to Buckingham Palace and see the King. But they had turned out a battalion of Guards and some of the ring leaders were arrested. Churchill was War Minister at this time and he told Parliament they would be severely dealt with. But most of the MP's were sympathetic towards the men. Then an order was issued to pay all men stranded in London 5 shillings a day and a bed. They should have thought of that sooner: it would have saved a lot of trouble. I went

home from Liverpool Street for another week, and when I went back some welfare officers met us with lorries to take us from Liverpool Street to Victoria. At Victoria Station everything was quiet and trains were waiting.

It was in an atmosphere of obvious gloom, therefore, that the War Cabinet on 12 February discussed the current position and the future prospects of the intervention in Russia. Churchill said that Britain's enterprises in all direction were 'crumbling'. The Bolsheviks were getting stronger every day. 'We ought to intervene.' Lloyd George said that this would mean sending at least 1 million men in the spring. Not on that scale, replied Churchill – but at least they should try to 'keep alive the Russian forces attempting to make headway against the Bolsheviks'. To this Lloyd George retorted:

> The Russian non-Bolshevik armies are inferior to the Bolsheviks neither in men nor guns, and if the Russian population had been behind them they would certainly have made headway. For months the Bolsheviks had none of the essentials of a disciplined army, yet the (non-Bolshevik) Russians had made no effective advance.

Successful intervention would require 500,000 men, and even if help with guns and equipment only were sent, at least 150,000 British soldiers would be required. Faced with this remorseless pressure, Churchill agreed that such large-scale intervention was impossible. The point was clinched by the Chancellor of the Exchequer: 'Noone believed that the non-Bolshevik Governments in Russia could by themselves stand for a moment'.[18]

'If demobilisation had been stopped in order to divert the troops from France to Odessa or Archangel there would have been a mutiny. The attempt to raise a force of volunteers for the purpose of waging war against the Bolsheviks was a miserable failure,' wrote Lloyd George himself concerning this period.[19]

From then onwards, in any case, the course of the British intervention in Russia was predetermined, despite all Churchill's efforts to steer it into the direction he favoured (the War Cabinet's minutes as well as his own papers furnish sufficient evidence of both). It became a gradually extinguished undertaking, in which the only outstanding military event was the despatch of a supplementary force to cover the withdrawal of the British forces in north Russia.

It was the determined action of the British soldiers which brought about the beginning of that fiasco, against the wishes of the War Cabinet and the politicians behind it, against the campaign of the newspaper proprietors and the interests behind them, and against the highest military authorities, unaccustomed to soldiers thinking for themselves about 'a political struggle of which they understood nothing'.

HOW BRITAIN DEMOBILISED

The statistics of discharges from the army are the practical confirmation of the changes brought about in the political plans of the authorities by those remarkable events of January 1919.

The British army at the end of the war numbered 625,000 officers and 5,973,000 men, according to a memorandum prepared by Sir Eric Geddes.[20] During the seven weeks between the Armistice and the end of December, 261,000 men had been demobilised – an average of 37,000 a week. As the result of the speeding-up which began in the second week of January, the numbers increased dramatically, and by the end of January nearly 1 million men had been demobilised. By the end of February the figure was 1,713,000; by the end of March 2,149,000; by the end of April 2,537,000; by the end of May 2,800,000. By the end of June it was 2,929,000, and by mid-December 1919 nearly 4 million men out of less than 6 million had been discharged.[21]

Whatever the War Cabinet's wishes may have been with regard to the intervention in Russia, there were not the forces for continuing it. And it was the men in khaki who had brought this about. Winston Churchill himself made a belated comment on this fact, in a world broadcast on 26 March 1944:

> At the time of the great demobilisation after the last war, in about six months we brought home from abroad, released from military service and restored to their families nearly 3,000,000 men. Great plans had been prepared before the Armistice by the planners to bring home all the key men first, and any soldier who could get a telegram from someone at home saying that he was wanted for a key job had priority over the man who had borne the burden and

heat of the war. The troops did not think this was fair, and by the time I went to the War Office a convulsion of indiscipline shook the whole of our splendid Army, which had endured unmoved all danger, slaughter and privation. I persuaded the Cabinet to reverse this foolish and inequitable plan, and substitute the simple rule 'First out first home', and the process of demobilisation went forward in a smooth and orderly fashion.[22]

Considering Churchill's desperate fight to have perhaps 500,000 experienced men, or more, in the armed forces at the beginning of 1919, with a view to destroying the Soviet Republic, his claims, twenty-five years later, about his own part may seem ludicrous. But he certainly put his finger on the essence of the thing when he said that 'the troops did not think this war fair'.

WHAT THE STRIKES DECIDED

In the records of Great Britain and the Soviet Republic there is a singular similarity in the views expressed by the farsighted leaders of their respective Governments.

On 16 January 1919, at the Allied Supreme Council, Lloyd George pointed out that the Germans,

> at the time when they needed every available man to reinforce their attack on the Western Front, had been forced to keep about a million men to garrison a few provinces of Russia which were a mere fringe of the whole country, and moreover at that time Bolshevism was weak and disorganised. Now it was strong and had a formidable army. Was anyone of the Western Allies prepared to send a million men into Russia? He doubted whether a thousand were willing to go. All reports tended to show that the Allied troops in Siberia and Northern Russia were most unwilling to continue the campaign and determined to return to their homes.

Referring to the Czechs, he said that they were unwilling to fight to set up another Tsarist régime, 'and so also were the British'.

At further conversations of the Allied Premiers with President Wilson, also in Paris, on 21 January 1919, Lloyd George added that 'He felt certain that, if the British tried to send any more troops there [to Russia], there would be mutiny'. None of these remarks were published at the time.[23]

Also on 21 January 1919, Lenin wrote (for publication immediately): 'Attempts to conquer Russia, which require a long-term occupation army of a million men, are the most certain road to the most rapid extension of proletarian revolution to the Entente countries'.[24]

That both statesmen hit upon the same figure is not surprising. Lloyd George had already put it forward in his challenges to Churchill in the War Cabinet. Lenin was speaking from his knowledge of the size and constantly increasing strength of the Red Army. And while the British soldiers who had been going on strike all over the country probably never gave a thought to it, they did understand the essential: that full-scale war on the Bolsheviks would require a huge army, sooner or later, and that without their assistance such a war was impossible.

Even the very fragmentary news of their demonstrations which reached Soviet Russia in those days – mostly through German or Scandinavian newspaper reports, or the interception of French wireless bulletins – was of course of the highest importance for that very reason. The minutes of the Moscow City Soviet – a body of well over 1000 delegates from factory, office, Red Army and housewives' meetings – at the beginning of 1919 are of great interest in this respect.

On 25 January 1919 L. B. Kamenev, its president, was explaining why the Allies, after months of invasion and assistance to Russian counter-revolutionary generals, had recently suggested a meeting on Prinkipo Island, which all the governments exercising effective authority in any part of the former Russian Empire should be invited to attend. He said:

> This is quite understandable, because after four years of slaughter it is now extremely difficult to force Italian, French and British soldiers to go and throttle the Russian revolution. All the information which reaches us is evidence, on the one hand, of a vast revolutionary movement, and on the other of a tremendous desire of the armies to go home, and not to go to the Black Sea and Archangel.

It will be noticed that there was no suggestion of the *soldiers* being inspired by revolutionary sentiments.

A fortnight later, on 11 February 1919, the City Soviet heard a report on the international situation by Maxim Litvinov, a long-term Bolshevik exile in Britain who had served as unrecognised Soviet representative in the United Kingdom after the October Revolution, then had been imprisoned when Bruce Lockhart was arrested in Moscow in September 1918, and had recently returned to Russia. In the course of his speech, Litvinov referred to the remarkable 'Hands Off Russia!' conference on 18 January, and continued:

> At that time soldiers' meetings were taking place, and the soldiers who were on leave were demanding immediate demobilisation instead of being sent to the front. They were electing delegates, holding meetings and putting up placards with the inscription, 'We won't go to Russia'. Encountering such goings-on in their own country, the Allied Governments naturally had to think over whether they could fulfil their plans by military force. They had to begin thinking about other methods . . . They cannot send large armies, large forces, for the simple reason that the soldiers refuse to go. But they continue secretly to support all counter-revolutionary activities in Russia.[25]

On this occasion, too, the *objective* importance of the soldiers' movement was emphasised, without any suggestion that they themselves were inspired by consciously revolutionary sentiments.

Lastly, there was an address by Fyodor Raskolnikov, the Bolshevik midshipman who in 1917 had been the chosen spokesman of the sailors of the Baltic fleet, and in 1918 Deputy People's Commissar for the navy and commander of the Soviet fleet on the Caspian. He was captured during a naval engagement with British gunboats, taken to England and held in Brixton Prison for several months before being exchanged. Very soon after his return he was invited, on 3 June 1919, to address the Moscow City Soviet. After a survey of the economic and political situation in Britain, he quoted at length the speech of Lloyd George in the House of Commons on 16 April 1919, warning that to send troops to Russia would mean opening the doors to Bolshevism in Britain, and advocating instead the despatch of material aid of every kind to the White governments, rather than direct intervention. But, Raskolnikov continued,

During the days when I was leaving England there was a lively discussion in the British press of the question of an attack by Finland on Petrograd. Both British and Russian Whites were demanding that the British Government should help not only with arms, war materials and food, but also with men. That is, they were demanding just that which the British Government is quite unable to give, because apart from a few miserable handfuls of volunteers, it is not in a position to move organised military units.[26]

The audience to which such words were addressed in the first half of 1919 – not only the deputies to the City Soviet but the hundreds of thousands of workmen, Red soldiers of the capital's garrison, housewives and office employees among whom the deputies worked and lived between sessions – were living on starvation rations: even industrial workers and children, the highest 'food category', were getting no more than half a pound of bread a day, with occasional issues of smoked fish or a few ounces of sugar. They worked, lived and even met at sessions of the Soviet in unheated buildings. Arthur Ransome and Philips Price[27] in their vivid descriptions of Russia in those days testified to the trials which this brought. Cut off by the White armies (well subsidised by their foreign backers), and from the great resources of foodstuffs and raw materials all round the borders of Central Russia, the Soviet Republic at the same time had to call on tens of thousands of its skilled industrial workers again and again to lead military units and organise local activities in the countryside, instead of repairing and maintaining factories which produced clothing and other consumer goods. The hardships of this struggle for the life of the new Socialist order far exceeded any which the soldiers of the invading foreign armies had left behind them.

It was with the most rapt attention and enthusiasm that the deputies listened to these speeches and carried their information back to the people – just because the information that the invasion from Britain (and France, as other returning emigrants and prisoners of war told) was breaking down at its very source brought a new certainty of victory before long, if they could only hold out.

At this point it is appropriate to point out another striking coincidence.

On 16 April Prime Minister Lloyd George had in fact made a lengthy statement on the Government's Russian policy to the House of Commons. He said:

Russia is a country which it is very easy to invade but very difficult to conquer. It has never been conquered by a foreign foe, although it has been successfully invaded many times. It is a country which it is easy to get into, but very difficult to get out of (laughter and cheers). If we conquered Russia – and we could conquer it – you would be surprised at the military advice which is given me as to the number of men which would be required, and I should like to know where they are to come from. Has anyone reckoned up what an Army of Occupation would cost in Russia? Members showed a natural anxiety to control the expenditure in this country on railways and canals. But Sir Eric Geddes with all his energy could not in a quarter of a century spend as much money on railways and canals in Britain as a single year of military enterprise in Russia would cost us (cheers). I would rather leave Russia Bolshevist until she sees her way out of it than see Britain bankrupt (cheers). That is the surest road to Bolshevism in Britain (cheers) . . . To attempt military intervention in Russia would be the greatest act of stupidity that any government could possibly commit.

Lloyd George went on to argue instead for sending equipment, not troops, to Denikin, Kolchak and 'General Kharkoff'!

In spite of the pretence that such aid to the Whites was 'not intervention', and in spite of the assurances with which the Prime Minister began his speech, that he hated Bolshevism and its 'crimes', the supporters of the Whites in the House of Commons were furious, while their mouthpiece, *The Times* itself, displayed its anger by repeatedly calling the speech in the leading article, in its headlines and in its report of the debate, Lloyd George's 'apologia'.[28]

It so happened that Lenin on the very same day addressed a conference of the Moscow railwaymen on the same subject – and drew conclusions not unlike those to which Lloyd George had been obliged to come:

> We know that after their victory over Germany the Allies still had their capital, their multi-million army, their fleet second to none. Immediately after the defeat of Germany they had every possibility of turning all their forces to conquering the Russian Soviet Republic. What they were undertaking in the south of Russia – their landing from the Black Sea, their occupation of

Odessa – all this was aimed by the Allied imperialists against the Soviet Government.

Yet what now, five months later? Had they not the military forces, the armies millions strong, a fleet? Why have they had to retreat in face of a badly-equipped army of Ukrainian workers and peasants? It was because disintegration is going on among their own troops, of which there is evidence in the information which has penetrated to us. That information has been confirmed. You can't with impunity wage war for four years over the division of the capitalists' profits. And now that they have defeated Wilhelm – on whom they threw all the blame – they are incapable of carrying on the war. We know that in the military sense the Entente countries could have been – and, strictly speaking, still are – immeasurably stronger than we are. But at the same time we say: they have lost the war against us. This is not merely our imagination, not just our enthusiasm, it has been proved by events in Ukraine. They cannot go on fighting after all countries have been tortured and exhausted by the war, when it is becoming obvious for everyone that the war is being continued only in order to preserve the power of capital over the working people . . . The Allies will have to conclude peace with us. They are relying on Kolchak, they calculate that food difficulties will overthrow the Soviet power; but we say, it won't come off . . . The Allies, French and British, have lost the campaign: they have realised that the insignificant forces which they dispose of can't carry on the war against the Soviet Republic.[29]

Curiously enough, it must have been at that very time, too, that George Bernard Shaw – one of the most determined opponents of the British government's international policies every year since 1914 – wrote a biting attack on intervention, based on the same remorseless logic as that deployed, each in his own fashion, by Lenin and Lloyd George. The article appeared in the issue of the *Labour Leader* dated 24 January 1919 (published on 22 January): which means that Shaw must have written it about 16–18 January. Its culminating point read:

> If we persist in making war on Russia to force Ivan to restore the Tsardom, we shall produce a political crisis compared with which that produced by the late war is a joke. If we continue our royalist

war on the Russian revolution, there will be genuine pro-Russianism in England. There will be millions of Englishmen, including all the best Englishmen, who, far from wanting Generals Kolchak and Denikin to win, will most ardently pray that they may be knocked into a cocked hat by the Bolshevist troops, even if, to our eternal disgrace, some of their soldiers may be English soldiers.

This article, incidentally, was quoted at some length in the little *Call* issued to the British soldiers on the Northern Front in Russia (14 September 1919).

When the soldiers went on strike in 1919 in so many places, all over the British Isles and elsewhere (possibly in many other places of which no record has yet emerged), they were not of course thinking of such far-reaching results as those pointed out by Lenin. It is very likely that only a minority among them openly declared that they wouldn't go to Russia – even though all of them would have more or less consciously felt that overhanging peril. Their actions, in those few weeks of January 1919, were not organised from any mythical centre of 'Bolshevik propaganda', and were not co-ordinated by any secret network of 'agitators', as military bureaucrats like General Feilding suspected. What the citizens in uniform wanted was, above all, to go home and get back to their jobs. That was their aim, and in that they succeeded on the whole. And that was the immediate, short-term importance of their action.

At the same time, they prevented the despatch of huge armed forces against the Soviet Republic at a critical moment of its existence. Thereby they ensured the collapse, and the destruction by the Red Army, of the puppet armies and puppet régimes created by the Western democracies – Britain, France and the United States – with the hope of destroying the first Socialist state, a country with its proletariat 'organised as the ruling class', in the words of Marx and Engels. Thereby, in turn, the Soviet Republic was enabled to proceed (not without further difficulties and sufferings imposed from without) to the building and development of a Socialist society. That was the ultimate and long-term contribution made by the soldiers' strikes.

Incidentally, the historic importance of that movement does not end even there. The strikes had their profound connection with the October Revolution in Russia itself. 'The German prisoners liberated from Russia by the treaty of Brest-Litovsk returned infected with the Lenin virus. In large numbers they refused to go again to the front,' wrote Winston Churchill.[30] And in the English edition of his war memoirs, Ludendorff, Chief of the German General Staff wrote:

> A decided deterioration in the army's morale resulted from the enrolment, after long leave, of soldiers returned from long captivity in Russia . . . Divisions removed from East to West . . . brought a bad morale and had an unfavourable effect on their fellows.[31]

It was these German armies, thus characterised by the most ruthless enemies of the Soviet Republic as well as of Socialism generally, which were decisively defeated in the final bloody battles on the Western Front between July and September 1918. And when British soldiers began saying that the job for which they had put on uniforms had been done, that it was time for them now to go home, and they wouldn't stay in the 'bloody army' for another 'bloody war', they were themselves paying an effective, if belated and unconscious, tribute to the October Revolution.

NOTES

1 CAB. 23/8, Minute 514.
2 C. E. Calwell, *The Life of Sir Henry Wilson* (London: 1927) pp. 161–2.
3 Ibid., p. 181.
4 CAB. 23/8, Minute 515.
5 Calwell, op. cit., p. 164.
6 R. Blake (ed.), *Private Papers of Douglas Haig* (London: 1952) p. 350.
7 M. Gilbert, *Winston S. Churchill*, IV (London: 1975) p. 234.
8 The letter to Chamberlain, Wilson's diary and the Lloyd George papers, are quoted by Gilbert, op. cit., p. 234.
9 Calwell, op. cit., pp. 183–6, and Blake, op. cit., p. 351.
10 CAB. 23/8, Minute 520 (28 January) memorandum appended, dated 17 January 1919.
11 Quoted by Gilbert from the Churchill papers.
12 Calwell, op. cit., p. 166.
13 Gilbert, op. cit., p. 235.
14 CAB. 23/8, Minute 521.
15 Calwell, op. cit., p. 167.
16 Gilbert, op. cit., pp. 237–8.
17 Calwell, op. cit., p. 169.
18 CAB. 23/8, Minute 531.

19 *The Truth About The Peace Treaties*, I (London: 1938) p. 319.
20 WO 32, 5248 (14 January 1919).
21 Figures given by *The Times*, on War Office authority, 31 January, 1 March, 29 March, 26 April, 29 May, 25 June and 22 December 1919. The figures in the official *Summaries of Military Events for 7 Days* (WO 106. 329 at the Public Record Office) coincide almost exactly with those of *The Times*.
22 *The War Speeches of the Rt. Hon. Winston S. Churchill*, III, compiled by Charles Eade (London: 1952) pp. 114–15.
23 *Foreign Relations of the United States: Russia* (Washington: 1919) pp. 12, 13, 23. This did not mean that the British Prime Minister was against all intervention in Russia. He still held (as shown earlier) to the original Cabinet decisions of December 1917, in so far as they applied to the sending of munitions, equipment and money to the Whites fighting the Bolsheviks, but he was against sending men.
24 'Letter to Workers of England and America' (published in *Pravda* and *Izvestia* on 24 January 1919).
25 A useful survey of Litvinov's speech at this meeting – though without the particular references to the British soldiers – was also given by the late Arthur Ransome in his *Six Weeks in Russia in 1919* (London: 1919) pp. 46–7.
26 These three passages are quoted from *Stenographic Reports of Sessions of the Moscow Council of Workers' and Red Army Deputies*, (Moscow: 1919) 13 January–10 June 1919 (in Russian), pp. 41, 46, 234–5.
27 M. Philips Price, *My Reminiscences of the Russian Revolution* (London: 1921).
28 *The Times*, 17 April 1919.
29 *Pravda*, 23 April 1919.
30 Winston Churchill, *The World Crisis*, III (London: 1938) Chapter 21.
31 Erich von Ludendorff, *War Memories*, II (London: 1919) pp. 642, 749.

Index

Allied offensives, July–November 1918, 1, 2
Anti-Bolsheviks, money for, 13, 22
Archangel
  Allied landing 2.8.18, 12
  puppet government there, 12
  Allied worries after Armistice, 21–2
  evacuation decided, March 1919, 79
  sentence on sergeants who led strike, 80
Armistice
  celebrations in Britain, 2, 3
  restraint among troops overseas, 2–5
  Germans to continue occupying Russian territory, 11–12
Austria
  Hungary, asks for armistice 27.10.18, 1
  Vienna revolution 3.11.18, 1

Balfour, A. J. (Foreign Secretary)
  Memorandum on Russia 21.12.18, 13
  report on intervention plans 18.10.18, 14.11.18, 22, 23
  suggests using German troops there, 23
  opposes evacuation of North Russia 10.12.18, 24
Banks, F. R.
  on sailor mechanics who wanted demobilisation, February 1919, 75
Bernard Shaw
  attack on intervention 24.2.19, 24, 104–5
Bottomley, Horatio, 10
Budapest
  workers' and soldiers' rising 30.10.18, 1

Bulgaria
  soldiers' rising 25.9.18, 1
  sues for peace 27.9.18, 1

Call
  (organ of British Socialist Party), 5, 7, 13–14
  (Soviet news-sheet in English for Allied forces in North Russia 1918–19), 76–8
Call-up on eve of Armistice 6.11.18, 11
Cecil, Lord Robert (Under-Secretary for Foreign Affairs)
  opposes withdrawal from Russia 18.10.18, 22
  supports aid for Whites 14.11.18, 23
Censorship, reimposed on soldiers 'strikes' reports 3.1.19, 40–1, 64–5
Chamberlain, Austen (Chancellor of the Exchequer)
  says Cabinet should not be influenced by questions at election meetings 10.12.18, 24–5
  anti-Bolshevik governments 'could not stand by themselves' 12.2.19, 97
Churchill, Winston (Minister of Munitions, later Secretary for War)
  wants German army built up again 10.11.18, 23
  Bolsheviks 'ferocious baboons' 26.11.18, 24
  Glasgow Herald on his appointment 11.1.19, 89
  fear of 'Bolshevism in Britain' 10.1.19, 93
  tells journalists anti-Bolshevik forces would 'crumble' without British troops 15.1.19, 94

Churchill, Winston (*contd.*)
  tells Chamberlain: Army 'liquefying fast' 16.1.19, 94
  unless demobilisation question settled, Army will become 'demoralised and angry mob' 19.1.19, 94
  admits 'orders would not be obeyed' if more troops sent to Russia 27.1.19, 95
  but presses again for more to be sent 28.1.19, 95
  broadcast claims, March 1944, 98–9 (in 1938) on German soldiers' morale in 1918, 105–6
Curzon, Lord (deputy to Balfour at Foreign Office)
  opposes withdrawal from Russia 10.12.18, 24
  but admits popular opposition to intervention, 24
  thinks volunteers for intervention not forthcoming 10.1.19, 93

Daily Chronicle, wants extended intervention 1.1.19, 2.1.19, 29, 30
Daily Express, bitter attacks on intervention policy and demobilisation delays 22.11.18 to 4.1.19, 31, 32–5
Daily Herald, prints British Consul's attack on intervention 14.12.18, 24
Daily Mail, attacks demobilisation delays 29.11.18 to 13.12.18, 31–2
Daily Telegraph campaigns for intervention 19.12.18, 1.1.19, 27, 29
Demobilisation
  only 108,000 men by 31.12.18, 25
  War Cabinet decides not to extend it to Russia 31.12.18, 25
  must wait (*Morning Post* 9.12.18; *The Times* 12.12.18; *Daily Chronicle* 1.1.19), 30
  statistics, January–December 1919, 98–9
Discontent among soldiers overseas, 33, 65–8

Economic conditions in wartime
  wages, cost of living, food queues, 5
  separation allowances, 6
  profits and dividends, 6–7

Fineberg, Joe (E.C. British Socialist Party: later editor of Soviet news-sheet *The Call*), 76

Gallacher, William, quoted, 7, 9
General Election 14.12.18, 6, 25, 27, 28–9
Generals' and commanding officers' talks with soldiers
  Folkestone, Dover, 38, 40
  Shortlands, 41–2
  Biggin Hill, 42
  Osterley Park, 43
  Grove Park, Upper Norwood, 44
  Fairlop, 45
  Park Royal, War Office, 46
  Shoreham, 48
  Winchester, Aldershot, 49
  Falmouth, 53
  Stonehenge, 57
  Harwich, 58
  Bedford, 58–9
  Kettering, 59
  Harlaxton, 60
  Heaton Park, 61
  Blackpool, Holywood, 62
  Cramlington, 63
  Calais, 69–70, 72–3
Germany, resistance up to November 1918, 1–2
  asks for armistice 5.10.18, 2
  navy revolts 3.11.18, 2
  delegation at Compiègne 8.11.18, 2
  suggestions to use troops against Bolsheviks (by Balfour, Sir Henry Wilson, Churchill), 23, 93–4
Guards battalions for Cologne stopped 4.1.19, 37

Haig, General Sir Douglas (C.I.C.)
  thinks (October 1918) Germans can still resist in 1919, 2
  wants to shoot Calais strikers, 70

INDEX

tells C.I.G.S. state of Army 'deplorable' 14.1.19, 94
says Army 'rapidly disappearing' 15.1.19, 94
prospect: 'no Army left in France by February', 22.1.19, 94

India
soldier's question to G.O.C. at Karachi (April 1919), 81
Intervention in (invasion of) Russia
origin and progress, 12
books on, 12, 15–16
pretexts for, before Armistice in West, 12, 21
continuation after Armistice, 12, 25, 29
British protests before Armistice in West, 13–14
British protests after Armistice, 14–15
pretexts for, after Armistice, 22–5, 27
Ireland, Home Rule Bill rejected (6.11.18), 11
Ironside, Major-General Sir Edmund (CIC North Russia)
his cables about soldiers' strikes on Archangel front 23.2.19, 27.2.19, 3.3.19, 78–9
description in his book, 79
thinks soldiers 'understood nothing' about politics of intervention, 80–1

Jackson, T. A. quoted, 9

Kamenev, L. B. (President, Moscow City Soviet)
on mood of British soldiers 25.1.19, 100
Karachi
soldiers paraded for service after Armistice, 81
Kiel, German naval revolt at 3.11.18, 2

Lenin, V. I.
letter to British and American workers, 21.1.19, 100
address to Moscow railwaymen 16.4.19, 103–4
Litvinov, M. M.
speech at Moscow City Soviet on British soldiers' protests 11.2.19, 101
Lloyd George, David (Prime Minister)
on danger from 'inflammable' British workers 19.11.18, 24
reads Bernard Shaw's letter at War Cabinet 10.12.18, 24
warns of possible Army discontent, 24
doubts if troops would go to suppress Bolshevism 31.12.18, 25
willing to meet striking soldiers 8.1.19, 91
warns Churchill of 'trouble in the Army' 18.1.19, 95
warns him again of 'considerable unrest' 3.2.19, 96
tells War Cabinet 'at least 1,000,000 men' needed for successful intervention 12.2.19, 97
gives similar warnings at Allied meetings in Paris 16.1.19, 21.1.19, 99–100
repeats them in House of Commons 16.4.19, 102–3
Lockhart, Robert Bruce
on fate of leaders of Archangel strike, 80
Ludendorff, General Erich von (Chief of German Imperial General Staff)
on morale of German troops in 1918, 106

Marcushevsky, General
on British soldiers' strike at Archangel, 85
Middle peasants in Russia
their role in Civil War, 17, 19
Milner, Lord (Secretary for War, 1918)
urges sending no more troops to Russia 14.11.18, 23–4
urges help for Whites in South Russia 18.11.18, 23–4
foretells 'massacre' if British troops withdraw 10.12.18, 24

Milner, Lord (*contd.*)
  notes 'difficulty' created by popular opposition, 24
  issues statement justifying intervention 18.12.18, 27
  opposes Premier meeting soldiers 8.1.19, 91
Morning Post wants Declaration of war on Soviet Russia 21.12.18, 31.12.18, 28
Moscow City Soviet, 100, 102

Nabokov, K. D. (White representative in London)
  report on political opposition to intervention 28.12.18, 26

Objections by soldiers to being sent to Russia
  Folkestone 4.1.19, 37
  Osterley Park 6.1.19, 44
  Park Royal 7.1.19, 46
  Aldershot 7.1.19, 49
  Bedford 5.1.19, 58
  Calais 30.1.19, 69
  admitted by press after soldiers' strikes began, 86–9
  Socialist press on, 89–91
  admitted by Sir Eric Geddes (First Lord of the Admiralty) 8.1.19, 92
  and by Sir Henry Wilson 10.1.19, 93

Pantley, Pte. John, R.A.O.C.
  arrested at Calais, 69, 71–2
  died of pneumonia, 73
'People's Russian Information Bureau', 14
Plan for 'Military Commitments after Peace' 6.12.18, 25
Pollitt, Harry, quoted, 10
Prague, insurrection 28.10.18, 1
Prinkipo Peace Conference
  proposal accepted by Soviet Government, 78
  Allied embarrassment, 84–5

Raskolnikov, F. F. (Deputy Navy Commissar)
  at Moscow City Soviet on British soldiers' protests 3.6.19, 101–2
Red Army, stages in its organisation, 1918, 18–19
Rhyl, Canadian mutiny at, 83
Robertson, General Sir William (GOC Home Forces)
  receives deputation from Park Royal 8.1.19, 46
  War Cabinet's decision on this, 92
Russia
  German occupation under Armistice terms 11.11.18, 11–12
  division into Allied 'zones of operation' 23.12.18, 13
  military and economic conditions after October Revolution, 17–20

Shop Stewards' movement, 7, 9, 14
Smuts, General J. C.
  on danger of Bolshevism 18.10.18, 22
Social contrasts in wartime, 7
Socialists, police action against, 10–11
Soldiers' strikes and demonstrations where:
  Folkestone, Dover, 37–40
  Shortlands, Maidstone, Biggin Hill, Richborough, 41–3
  Osterley Park, Grove Park, Uxbridge, Kempton Park, Fairlop, White City, Upper Norwood, Park Royal, 43–6
  Shoreham, Aldershot, 47–49
  Salonika, 47, 68
  Winchester, East Liss, Beaulieu, Freshwater, 49–50
  Bristol, Falmouth, 51, 53
  Larkhill, Stonehenge, 54–57
  Felixstowe, Bedford, Kettering, Harlaxton, Leeds, Kilnsea, 58–61
  Heaton Park, Blackpool, Holywood, Cramlington, 61–3
  Edinburgh, Leith, Stirling, Cromarty, 63–4
  Worghams le Petit, Beauvais, Calais, 68–73
  Etaples, le Havre, Dunkirk, 73–5

Archangel, 78–81
units involved:
Army Service Corps, 39, 41, 43, 44, 46–7, 49, 52, 59, 61
Royal Garrison Artillery, 39, 48
Royal Engineers, 39, 49, 54–7, 58–9
The Queens Regiment, 3rd Battn. Glosters, 3rd Battn. Wiltshires, 42
Royal Air Force, 43, 50, 52, 58, 60, 62–3
Armament School, 44
Army Pay Corps, 44
Royal Army Ordnance Corps, 44, 45, 49, 69–73
Royal Marine Engineers, 48
London and Eastern Command Depots, 48–9
Siege Artillery Reserve Brigade, 48–9
12th Battn. Bedfordshires, 51–2
25th Battn. Rifle Brigade, 52
3rd Res. Battn. King's Own Yorkshire Light Infantry, 61
562nd Home Employment Coy., 61
Royal Army Medical Corps., 61–2
3rd Battn. Somerset Regt., 62
Highland Light Infantry, 63
Scottish Rifles, 63
459th Agricultural Coy., 63
3rd Battn. Seaforth Highlanders, 64
13th Battn. Yorkshire Regt., 78–80, 85
in the Navy:
Milford Haven, 52
Plymouth, 52–3
Devonport, 53
Liverpool, 62
Rosyth, 63–4
'at sea', 75–6
South Slavs, proclaim independence 29.10.18, 1
Southampton, events reported at, 50–1
Soviet Russia 1918
military problems, 17–18
economic problems, 19–20
social reforms, 20
peace offers, 20–1

The Times newspaper
articles supporting intervention 1918, 14.11, 29.11, 18.12, 28.12, 27
1919, 4.1, 29–30
attacks Lloyd George for not extending intervention 17.1.19, 103
Trenchard, Major-General Hugh Montague, 50–1

Victoria Station, scenes at, February 7 1919, 96–7

War Cabinet
decides to support any anti-Bolshevik force in Russia, November 1917, 13
alarm when soldiers' strikes began, 91
War casualties
British, 2
French, 2
White armies in Russia
formed 1918, 17–19
at Archangel after August 1918, 85
Wilson, General Sir Henry (Chief of Imperial General Staff)
disturbing report from Archangel 18.10.18, 22
danger was 'Bolshevism, not Boche' 9.11.18, 23.
plans continued intervention after peace 6.12.18, 25
thinks Premier wants to evacuate Murmansk to gain votes 10.12.18, 25
secures War Cabinet approval of his plans 12.12.18, 25
denounces press attacks on military authorities 14.1.19, 67
Premier's meeting soldiers would be 'disastrous' 8.1.19, 91
fears Army will become a 'rabble' 6.1.19, 92
urges Premier to 'crush out poisonous press' 7.1.19, 92
admits intervention 'immensely un-

Wilson, General Sir Henry (*contd.*)
  popular' among soldiers 10.1.19, 93
  tells Churchill: 'sitting on a mine' 17.1.19, 94
  thinks Army discipline 'a thing of the past' 22.1.19, 94

'Workers' and Soldiers' Council' (Leeds: 1917), 9

Young, Douglas (British Consul, Archangel)
  article attacking British policy in Russia 14.12.18, 24